GREAT DAYS IN HISTORY

THE UNFOLDING OF THE SCHEME OF REDEMPTION

Andy Sochor

Gospel Armory
PUBLISHING

Great Days in History: The Unfolding of the Scheme of Redemption

Published by:
Gospel Armory Publishing
Bowling Green, Kentucky
www.GospelArmory.com

Printed in the United States of America

ISBN: 978-1-942036-28-9

To Him be the glory, both now and
to the day of eternity. Amen.

2 Peter 3:18

TABLE OF CONTENTS

Great Days in History

Introduction

If we look back through history, it is easy to see that the level of freedom we have enjoyed in the United States since the founding of the nation is certainly not typical. Those of us who have only lived under such blessed conditions often find it difficult to comprehend living in a society in which the people do not enjoy freedom, especially when we realize that the vast majority of mankind has not enjoyed the liberties that we have as American citizens. The fact that a free society such as ours exists – and has continued as long as it has – is truly remarkable.

We might wonder what had to happen in order for the principles of freedom to take root and flourish in the West generally and in the United States specifically. In the book, *7 Tipping Points that Saved the World,*[1] authors Chris Stewart and Ted Stewart highlighted seven events in human history that were critical to the birth and development of a free society. Had the outcomes of any of these events been different, our generation may have never known the freedoms we know now.

Throughout history, there have been pivotal events that have vastly altered the futures of individuals, tribes, nations,

---

[1] Chris Stewart and Ted Stewart, *The Miracle of Freedom: 7 Tipping Points that Saved the World* (Shadow Mountain, 2011).

and civilizations. The present has been shaped by the past with certain events being especially monumental.

While we might appreciate the great benefit of liberty and the advantage of living in a free society, there is something else that is far more important – eternal redemption and salvation from sin. Just as the blessing of freedom was made possible for us by several key events throughout history, the gift of salvation was brought about by several key events in which God carried out His scheme of redemption.

In this series of lessons, we are going to examine these *great days in history* – not in secular history, but days of spiritual importance – in order to help us appreciate and take advantage of God's plan to bring us home with Him in heaven for eternity.

GREAT DAYS IN HISTORY

1

THE DAY OF CREATION

"In the beginning God created the heavens and the earth" (Genesis 1:1).

"This is the account of the heavens and the earth when they were created, in the day that the Lord God made earth and heaven" (Genesis 2:4).

In this first lesson, we are going to go all the way back to the beginning – to the *day of Creation*. What happened on that day? What lessons do we need to learn from it?

The Background

God is eternal – If we begin with the Creation of the world, how can we go back further than that? When it comes to the history of this world, there is nothing further back – this was the beginning point. However, while this was the beginning of the *creation*, it was not the beginning of the *Creator*. God existed prior to the creation of the universe.

> *"Before the mountains were born or You gave birth to the earth and the world, even from everlasting to everlasting, You are God"* (Psalm 90:2).
>
> *"Your throne is established from of old; You are from everlasting"* (Psalm 93:2).

When Jesus prayed to the Father, He said, *"Now, Father, glorify Me together with Yourself, with the glory which I had with You before the world was"* (John 17:5). Later in the same prayer, He said, *"For You loved Me before the foundation of the world"* (John 17:24). While the creation had a beginning point, God Himself has no beginning. When He appeared to Moses in the burning bush, He said, *"I AM WHO I AM...Thus you shall say to the sons of Israel, 'I AM has sent me to you'"* (Exodus 3:14). He identified Himself as *"I AM."* This means He simply exists. He has always been and will always be.

God had a plan – The creation of the universe was not a spur-of-the-moment decision or an off-the-cuff type of endeavor. God determined to have a people for Himself, and this determination was made *before* He began creating the heavens and the earth. Paul wrote, *"He chose us in Him before the foundation of the world, that we would be holy and blameless before Him"* (Ephesians 1:4).

In fact, God even knew that having His own special people would require His Son to have to die on the cross. Jesus was described as *"the Lamb slain from the foundation of the world"* (Revelation 13:8, NKJV). We are God's people after having been redeemed by the blood of Christ (Ephesians 1:7). Even before the world was formed, the scheme of redemption had already been planned in the mind of God.

A point to remember – Keep in mind that the "day" of Creation includes the entire Creation week. While the text of Genesis 1 indicates that the days were literal, consecutive, 24-hour days, the term was used differently in the next chapter: *"This is the account of the heavens and the earth when they were created, in the* ***day*** *that the Lord God made earth and heaven"* (Genesis 2:4). In this verse, the "day" of Creation includes all six days of the Creation week in which He made the universe and everything in it. So we are not just looking at "Day 1" of creation; instead, we are considering all that God did in creating *"the heavens and the earth"* (Genesis 1:1).

The Events on That Day

God spoke the universe into existence – One of the remarkable facts about the Creation is that everything that was created was made when *"God said"* they were to be made (Genesis 1:3, 6, 9, 11, 14, 20, 24, 26). The psalmist emphasized this:

> *"By the word of the Lord the heavens were made, and by the breath of His mouth all their host. He gathers the waters of the sea together as a heap; He lays up the deeps in storehouses. Let all the earth fear the Lord; let all the inhabitants of the world stand in awe of Him. For He spoke, and it was done; He commanded, and it stood fast"* (Psalm 33:6-9).

When John began his gospel record, he began with the same words as the author of Genesis: *"In the beginning..."* (John 1:1; Genesis 1:1). John started by introducing Jesus as the Word: *"In the beginning was the Word, and the Word was with God, and the Word was God. He was in the beginning with God. All things came into being through Him, and apart from Him nothing came into being that has come into being"* (John 1:1-3). Jesus was credited with creating all things. Paul wrote, *"For by Him all things were created, both in the heavens and on earth, visible and invisible, whether thrones or dominions or rulers or authorities—all things have been created through Him and for Him"* (Colossians 1:16). This one who created all things, who spoke all things into existence, was *"the Word* [who] *became flesh"* (John 1:14). When the Scriptures discuss the Creation, an emphasis is placed upon the power of God's word.

God created the world in an orderly manner – The first chapter of Genesis explained what God created on each of the six days of Creation. However, it was not just that He made something different on each day; there was a pattern to the six days.

- The creation of *light* on the **first** day (Genesis 1:3-5) corresponded to the creation of the *lights* on the **fourth** day (Genesis 1:14-19).
- The creation of the *sea and sky* on the **second** day (Genesis 1:6-8) corresponded to the creation of the *sea life and birds* on the **fifth** day (Genesis 1:20-23).
- The creation of *land and vegetation* on the **third** day (Genesis 1:9-13) corresponded to the creation of *land animals and man* on the **sixth** day (Genesis 1:24-27).

God could have created everything instantly, yet He created the world in stages. By doing this, He showed Himself to be a God of order and patterns. This is why, even today, God expects His people to worship *"properly and in an orderly manner"* (1 Corinthians 14:40) and to *"hold fast the pattern"* that is found in His word (2 Timothy 1:13, NKJV).

God finished His creation – After the six days in which God created the heavens and earth and everything in it – which comprised the *"day"* of Creation (Genesis 2:4) – God's work in Creation was *"completed"* (Genesis 2:1). He then provided the basis for the Sabbath law (Exodus 20:8-11) that would be given later: *"By the seventh day God completed His work which He had done, and He rested on the seventh day from all His work which He had done. Then God blessed the seventh day and sanctified it, because in it He rested from all His work which God had created and made"* (Genesis 2:2-3). God was able to rest from His work because the Creation was completed.

This is significant because it shows us that God's work of creation is not ongoing. God is not out creating new species that did not previously exist, crafting new features into the earth that were not there before, or forming new men and women in the way that He did with Adam and Eve. His work in creating the universe was *"very good"* (Genesis 1:31). It did not (does not) need to be redone.

Key Lessons

God's power – The psalmist indicated that the physical creation serves as a witness to the existence and power of God: *"The heavens are telling of the glory of God; and their expanse is declaring the work of His hands"* (Psalm 19:1). Paul made a similar point in his letter to the Romans:

> *"For since the creation of the world His invisible attributes, His eternal power and divine nature,*

> *have been clearly seen, being understood through what has been made, so that they are without excuse"* (Romans 1:20).

For all of man's knowledge, wisdom, and technological advancements, no one is out creating new universes. No one can come close to matching God's *"eternal power"* that was on display in His creation of the world. Furthermore, none of it was done by accident. He had a plan and perfectly executed that plan. The creation followed a particular order; and when He was finished, it was *"very good"* (Genesis 1:31).

God's providence – The fact that God's work in creation could be *finished* highlights His *providence*. After discussing Jesus' role in creation (Colossians 1:16), Paul wrote, *"He is before all things, and in Him all things hold together"* (Colossians 1:17). The Greek word translated *"hold together"* or *"consist"* (KJV) is the same word that is translated *"formed"* in 2 Peter 3:5 – *"For when they maintain this, it escapes their notice that by the word of God the heavens existed long ago and the earth was formed out of water and by water."* God *"formed"* this world and because of the perfect way in which He formed it, everything is held together as it needs to be.

In this perfect creation, God's providence is ongoing. The psalmist made this point: *"Your faithfulness continues throughout all generations; You established the earth, and it stands. They stand this day according to Your ordinances, for all things are Your servants"* (Psalm 119:90-91). Because God's word is *"forever... settled in heaven"* (Psalm 119:89) and this word was used to bring about the physical world around us (Psalm 33:6-9), His faithfulness continues to be on display for all to see. This was what Paul meant when he told the residents of Lystra that God *"did not leave Himself without witness, in that He did good and gave you rains from heaven and fruitful seasons, satisfying your hearts with food and gladness"* (Acts 14:17). God's ongoing providence is a witness to His existence and care for mankind.

After the flood, God made Noah this promise: *"While the earth remains, seedtime and harvest, and cold and heat, and summer and winter, and day and night shall not cease"* (Genesis 8:22). To this day, God's promise is still being carried out. Even the mockers in Peter's day acknowledged this, though they failed to appreciate the significance of it: *"Where is the promise of His coming? For ever since the fathers fell asleep, all continues just as it was from the beginning of creation"* (2 Peter 3:4). These mockers were citing the fact that *"all continues just as it was"* as the reason why they doubted the promise of Christ's return. In other words, they saw the ongoing providence of God but completely missed the point. God was keeping His promise that the earth would continue in its regular seasons and cycles; therefore, they (and we) could be assured that He will keep His promise that Christ would return. *"All continues just as it was"* (2 Peter 3:4) because that was how God designed this world to function. It will continue to work this way as long as *"the earth remains"* (Genesis 8:22).

God's image – Man was made in the image of God: *"Then God said, 'Let Us make man in Our image, according to Our likeness; and let them rule over the fish of the sea and over the birds of the sky and over the cattle and over all the earth, and over every creeping thing that creeps on the earth.' God created man in His own image, in the image of God He created him; male and female He created them"* (Genesis 1:26-27). The fact that we have been made in God's image means that humans have a *spiritual* nature. Notice what the wise man wrote:

> *"For the fate of the sons of men and the fate of beasts is the same. As one dies so dies the other; indeed, they all have the same breath and there is no advantage for man over beast, for all is vanity. All go to the same place. All came from the dust and all return to the dust. Who knows that the breath of man ascends upward and the breath of the beast descends downward to the earth?"* (Ecclesiastes 3:19-21).

As the wise man focused on life *"under the sun"* (Ecclesiastes 1:9; 2:17; 3:16; *et al.*), he described the similarity between men and animals – both live and die and their bodies return to the earth. However, there is a significant difference between them – at death, man's spirit (breath) *"ascends upward"* while the animal's *"descends downward."* From an earthly perspective, there is no perceivable difference between the death of men and the death of animals. However, after death there is a difference. In the case of humans – beings who have been made in the image of God (Genesis 1:26-27) – our spirits *"return to God"* (Ecclesiastes 12:7).

This makes man unique. We are not highly evolved animals as the evolutionist believes; we occupy a special place in the Creation. David wrote, *"When I consider Your heavens, the work of Your fingers, the moon and stars, which You have ordained; what is man that You take thought of him, and the son of man that You care for him? Yet You have made him a little lower than God, and You crown him with glory and majesty"* (Psalm 8:3-5). Because we have been made in the likeness of God, He cares for us in a way that goes far beyond how He cares for the rest of His physical Creation. It extends into eternity after our lives on earth are over.

Conclusion

God created this world and all of the good things to enjoy in it. This shows us His power and His care for us. However, this world and our lives in it are only temporary. So God made a plan whereby we could be with Him eternally. In order to take advantage of this, we need to be sure we fulfill the purpose for which we were created.

> *"The conclusion, when all has been heard, is: fear God and keep His commandments, because this applies to every person. For God will bring every act to judgment, everything which is hidden, whether it is good or evil"* (Ecclesiastes 12:13-14).

As this world stands *"according to* [His] *ordinances"* (Psalm 119:91), we must continue to obey His instructions today.

Questions for Discussion and Reflection

1. How do we know that God had a plan to save us before He created the world?

2. Is the work of Creation ongoing?

3. What does the physical world tell us about God?

4. What does God's ongoing providence show about His attitude toward mankind?

5. How did God make man unique from the rest of the life He created?

GREAT DAYS IN HISTORY

2

THE DAY OF JESUS' BIRTH

> *"And I will put enmity between you and the woman, and between your seed and her seed; he shall bruise you on the head, and you shall bruise him on the heel"* (Genesis 3:15).

> *"But when the fullness of the time came, God sent forth His Son, born of a woman, born under the Law"* (Galatians 4:4).

After considering the day of Creation, we will now be moving to the *day of Jesus' birth*. This may seem like a big jump from the first day; however, we are not skipping the Old Testament. Instead, the Old Testament is the foundation for this lesson.

The Background

The fall – This was when sin was introduced into the world. God had given Adam clear instructions regarding what was prohibited: *"From any tree of the garden you may eat freely;*

but from the tree of the knowledge of good and evil you shall not eat, for in the day that you eat from it you will surely die" (Genesis 2:16-17). Eve also understood the prohibition, as she was able to explain it to the serpent when he questioned her about God's command: *"From the fruit of the trees of the garden we may eat; but from the fruit of the tree which is in the middle of the garden, God has said, 'You shall not eat from it or touch it, or you will die'"* (Genesis 3:2-3). Satan tempted her by twisting God's words, promising a benefit for violating God's law and claiming the punishment was nothing to be feared.

> *"The serpent said to the woman, 'You surely will not die! For God knows that in the day you eat from it your eyes will be opened, and you will be like God, knowing good and evil.' When the woman saw that the tree was good for food, and that it was a delight to the eyes, and that the tree was desirable to make one wise, she took from its fruit and ate, and she gave also to her husband with her, and he ate. Then the eyes of both of them were opened, and they knew that they were naked; and they sewed fig leaves together and made themselves loin coverings"* (Genesis 3:4-7).

As a result of this, the perfect world in which Adam and Eve lived became marred by sin. Notice the changes that took place because of this event:

- Immediately after completing the sixth day of Creation, God declared that *"all that He had made...was very good"* (Genesis 1:31). After sin came into the world, the ground was *"cursed"* (Genesis 3:17).
- Prior to the fall, Adam and Eve enjoyed

fellowship with God. There were times when *"the Lord God* [was] *walking in the garden in the cool of the day"* (Genesis 3:8), which would have been a welcome visit in the beginning. After the fall, they were separated from God as He *"drove the man out"* of the Garden and prevented him from returning. (Genesis 3:24).

- Before their sin, Adam and Eve had access to the tree of life. In the Garden they were able to *"stretch out* [their] *hand, and take...from the tree of life, and eat, and live forever"* (Genesis 3:22; cf. 2:9). Because they sinned, they would die. God had previously warned Adam of this: *"But from the tree of the knowledge of good and evil you shall not eat, for in the day that you eat from it you will surely die"* (Genesis 2:17). After he sinned, God reminded Adam that this would be his fate: *"By the sweat of your face you will eat bread, till you return to the ground, because from it you were taken; for you are dust, and to dust you shall return"* (Genesis 3:19).

In response to these changes that came about because of sin, God prophesied of the coming of Christ. Speaking to the serpent, He said, *"And I will put enmity between you and the woman, and between your seed and her seed; He shall bruise you on the head, and you shall bruise him on the heel"* (Genesis 3:15). From the beginning, the day of Jesus' birth was part of God's plan.

The promise to Abraham – The fulfillment of the prophecy regarding the seed of woman was given as a promise to Abraham: *"In your seed all the nations of the earth* *shall be blessed, because you have obeyed My voice"* (Genesis 22:18). All nations being blessed through his seed looked forward to Christ. This was made clear by both Peter and Paul (Acts 3:24-26; Galatians 3:16). The Law of Moses was given as a *"tutor to lead us to Christ"* (Galatians 3:24). All of the Old Testament was given in anticipation of the arrival of the Messiah who would save man from sin.

However, the promise to Abraham was more than just that all nations would be blessed through his seed (Genesis 22:18). The Lord also told him, *"Kings will come forth from you"* (Genesis 17:6). David was given a promise regarding his descendants that contained a prophecy of the reign of Christ: *"When your days are complete and you lie down with your fathers, I will raise up your descendant after you, who will come forth from you, and I will establish his kingdom. He shall build a house for My name, and I will establish the throne of his kingdom forever"* (2 Samuel 7:12-13). This is why many Old Testament prophecies – some of which have been included in this lesson – described the Messiah as a king who would descend from David. All of this was related to God's promise to Abraham.

Paul wrote, *"But when the fullness of the time came, God sent forth His Son, born of a woman, born under the Law, so that He might redeem those who were under the Law, that we might receive the adoption as sons"* (Galatians 4:4-5). Jesus would be born into the world to fulfill the prophecy made in the Garden in the beginning and to complete the promise made to Abraham that through his *"seed all the nations of the earth shall be blessed"* (Genesis 22:18).

Preserving a remnant – The Old Testament is a history of God's dealings with the descendants of Abraham –

particularly through Isaac and Jacob – leading to the fulfillment of the promise. The people were often punished for their disobedience, yet they were never completely destroyed. Notice the prophecy of Jeremiah:

> *"'Then I Myself will gather the remnant of My flock out of all the countries where I have driven them and bring them back to their pasture, and they will be fruitful and multiply. [...] Behold, the days are coming,' declares the Lord, 'When I will raise up for David a righteous Branch; and He will reign as king and act wisely and do justice and righteousness in the land. In His days Judah will be saved, and Israel will dwell securely; and this is His name by which He will be called, "The Lord our righteousness"'"* (Jeremiah 23:3-6).

While there are many noteworthy events that have been recorded in the Old Testament that provide valuable lessons for us (cf. Romans 15:4; 1 Corinthians 10:6, 11), this is the point we need to emphasize for our study. As all of the events were unfolding among the Jewish people, despite their disobedience, a remnant was preserved so that the promise to send Christ could be fulfilled. This would make salvation from sin available to the people of Judah and Israel (Jeremiah 23:6) as well as all of the nations (Isaiah 2:2-4; 62:1-2).

The Events on That Day

Jesus was born into humble circumstances – When Jesus was born, He was *"wrapped...in cloths, and laid...in a manger, because there was no room for them in the inn"* (Luke 2:7). We know that the family into which He was born was poor because they offered *"a sacrifice according to what was said in the Law of the Lord, 'A pair of turtledoves or two young pigeons'"* (Luke 2:24) – a provision for those who were too poor to afford a lamb for this sacrifice (Leviticus 12:8). Jesus was born in Bethlehem (Luke 2:4) – a town that was *"too little"* to be considered significant (Micah 5:2). He was raised in Nazareth (Matthew 2:23; Luke 2:39-40) – a town that was generally viewed with contempt (John 1:46).

If Jesus left the riches of heaven for the riches of earth, that would be a significant sacrifice since the *"treasures in heaven"* are far more valuable than any *"treasures on earth"* (Matthew 6:19-21; cf. 16:26). Yet Jesus did more than this. While on the earth, He had *"nowhere to lay His head"* (Luke 9:58). Paul wrote, *"For you know the grace of our Lord Jesus Christ, that though He was rich, yet for your sake He became poor, so that you through His poverty might become rich"* (2 Corinthians 8:9). Before we even consider His crucifixion, we can see Jesus' willingness to sacrifice for us in the fact that He was born into this world in the first place.

Prophecies concerning Jesus – There were several prophecies before and after the birth of Christ that announced the significance of this event.

- To Mary – *"The angel said to her, 'Do not be afraid, Mary; for you have found favor with God. And behold, you will conceive in your womb and bear a son, and you shall name Him Jesus. He will be great and will be called the Son of the Most High; and the Lord God will give Him the throne of His father David; and He will reign over the house of Jacob forever, and His kingdom will have no end'"* (Luke 1:30-33).

- To Joseph – *"But when he had considered this, behold, an angel of the Lord appeared to him in a dream, saying, 'Joseph, son of David, do not be afraid to take Mary as your wife; for the Child who has been conceived in her is of the Holy Spirit. She will bear a Son; and you shall call His name Jesus, for He will save His people from their sins.' Now all this took place to fulfill what was spoken by the Lord through the prophet: 'Behold, the virgin shall be with child and shall bear a Son, and they shall call His name Immanuel,' which translated means, 'God with us'"* (Matthew 1:20-23; cf. Isaiah 7:14; 9:6-7).
- To the shepherds – *"In the same region there were some shepherds staying out in the fields and keeping watch over their flock by night. And an angel of the Lord suddenly stood before them, and the glory of the Lord shone around them; and they were terribly frightened. But the angel said to them, 'Do not be afraid; for behold, I bring you good news of great joy which will be for all the people; for today in the city of David there has been born for you a Savior, who is Christ the Lord. This will be a sign for you: you will find a baby wrapped in cloths and lying in a manger'"* (Luke 2:8-12).
- To those in the temple (Simeon and Anna) – *"And there was a man in Jerusalem whose name was Simeon; and this man was righteous and devout, looking for the consolation of Israel; and the Holy Spirit was upon him. And it had been revealed to him by the Holy Spirit that he would*

> *not see death before he had seen the Lord's Christ. And he came in the Spirit into the temple; and when the parents brought in the child Jesus, to carry out for Him the custom of the Law, then he took Him into his arms, and blessed God, and said, 'Now Lord, You are releasing Your bond-servant to depart in peace, according to Your word; for my eyes have seen Your salvation, which You have prepared in the presence of all peoples, a light of revelation to the Gentiles, and the glory of Your people Israel"* (Luke 2:25-32; cf. Isaiah 9:1-2). *"And there was a prophetess, Anna the daughter of Phanuel, of the tribe of Asher. She was advanced in years and had lived with her husband seven years after her marriage, and then as a widow to the age of eighty-four. She never left the temple, serving night and day with fastings and prayers. At that very moment she came up and began giving thanks to God, and continuing to speak of Him to all those who were looking for the redemption of Jerusalem"* (Luke 2:36-38).

Through these prophecies, God was indicating that Jesus was the fulfillment of the prophecy in the Garden, the realization of the promise to Abraham, and the reason why the nation had been preserved throughout generations.

Honor was given to Jesus – Wise men from the east came to worship Jesus after He was born: *"Now after Jesus was born in Bethlehem of Judea in the days of Herod the king, magi from the east arrived in Jerusalem, saying, 'Where is He who has been born King of the Jews? For we saw His star in the east and have come to worship Him'"* (Matthew 2:1-2). When they saw Him, *"they fell* *to the ground and worshiped Him* [and] *presented to Him gifts of gold, frankincense, and myrrh"* (Matthew 2:11).

Key Lessons

God's promise – As we noticed in the previous lesson, the plan to send Jesus predated Creation (Revelation 13:8). However, the promise was first given in the Garden of Eden (Genesis 3:15) – in the beginning. The promise was also given to Abraham (Genesis 22:18) – centuries before Jesus' birth. There are other prophecies contained in the Old Testament regarding Jesus. Notice just a couple of these that relate to the birth of Jesus:

> *"Therefore the Lord Himself will give you a sign: Behold, a virgin will be with child and bear a son, and she will call His name Immanuel"* (Isaiah 7:14).

> *"For a child will be born to us, a son will be given to us; and the government will rest on His shoulders; and His name will be called Wonderful Counselor, Mighty God, Eternal Father, Prince of Peace. There will be no end to the increase of His government or of peace, on the throne of David and over his kingdom, to establish it and to uphold it with justice and righteousness from then on and forevermore. The zeal of the Lord of hosts will accomplish this"* (Isaiah 9:6-7).

> *"But as for you, Bethlehem Ephrathah, too little to be among the clans of Judah, from you One will go forth for Me to be ruler in Israel. His goings forth are from long ago, from the days of eternity"* (Micah 5:2).

These passages show us not only that Jesus would be born, but that He would be unique. His arrival into the world would be miraculous; He would be different from everyone else who had been or would be born into this world; and His life's work would not limited or stopped by death.

When God makes a promise, He keeps it. Paul told the saints in Rome, *"For whatever was written in earlier times was written for our instruction, so that through perseverance and the encouragement of the Scriptures we might have hope"* (Romans 15:4). When we study the Old Testament, we can be encouraged by the fact that God does what He says He will do. The Hebrew writer cited God's promise and oath to Abraham as *"two unchangeable things"* which guaranteed the promise, providing us with *"strong encouragement to take hold of the hope set before us"* (Hebrews 6:17-18).

When we consider Jesus' birth – in addition to all of the prophecies that were fulfilled by Him – we can see that God keeps His promises. Therefore, we can trust Him.

God's love – The love of God motivated Him to send Jesus into the world: *"For God so loved the world, that He gave His only begotten Son, that whoever believes in Him shall not perish, but have eternal life"* (John 3:16). Sin ruined man's relationship with God (Genesis 3:8, 23-24). Sadly, man continues to sin. *"For all have sinned and fall short of the glory of God"* (Romans 3:23). Adam introduced sin into the world by violating the law of God, then *"all sinned"* by following his example (Romans 5:12).

Rather than rejecting us forever, God wants to save us (John 3:16). Peter said that God *"is patient toward you, not wishing for any to perish but for all to come to repentance"* (2 Peter

3:9). Forgiveness of sins is available through the blood which Jesus shed on the cross (Ephesians 1:7). Sending Jesus to die for us demonstrates the great love that God has for us: *"But God demonstrates His own love toward us, in that while we were yet sinners, Christ died for us"* (Romans 5:8).

Jesus' humanity – When Jesus came to earth, He *"partook"* of *"flesh and blood"* (Hebrews 2:14). He took on the *"form of a bond-servant"* in order to be able to die on the cross (Philippians 2:5-8). Yet while on the earth, He was still God in the flesh. Paul explained, *"For in Him all the fullness of Deity dwells in bodily form"* (Colossians 2:9).

When Jesus lived in the flesh among men, He left a perfect example for us. Peter wrote, *"For you have been called for this purpose, since Christ also suffered for you, leaving you an example for you to follow in His steps, who committed no sin, nor was any deceit found in His mouth"* (1 Peter 2:21-22). By going through this, He proved that He can sympathize with us. Notice what the Hebrew writer said about this:

> *"Therefore, He had to be made like His brethren in all things, so that He might become a merciful and faithful high priest in things pertaining to God, to make propitiation for the sins of the people. For since He Himself was tempted in that which He has suffered, He is able to come to the aid of those who are tempted"* (Hebrews 2:17-18).

> *"For we do not have a high priest who cannot sympathize with our weaknesses, but One who has been tempted in all things as we are, yet without sin"* (Hebrews 4:15).

As the Creator (John 1:3), Jesus did not come to earth in a position of ignorance, needing to find out what it is like for man to experience the hardships and temptations of life. As the omniscient Creator, He already knew what we endure and how our minds respond to such things. Instead, Jesus came to show us that He understands all of this in order to prove to us that He can sympathize with us and to demonstrate that it is worth every effort to defeat sin and please God. Seeing His example, we should respond by following Him.

Conclusion

God's plan from before the Creation was to send Jesus into this world (Ephesians 1:4; Revelation 13:8). Despite our sin, God loved us and wanted to save us; but this required His Son to come to earth and die on the cross. Jesus' arrival proved that God cares for us and is willing to do whatever it takes to redeem us.

Questions for Discussion and Reflection

1. What event prompted God to make the first prophecy of the coming of Christ?

2. In what way was Jesus the fulfillment to the promise God made to Abraham?

3. What prophecies were made shortly before and after the birth of Jesus?

4. What characteristic of God prompted Him to send Jesus into this world?

5. According to the Hebrew writer, why did Jesus need to come in the flesh?

3

THE DAY OF JESUS' CRUCIFIXION

"Wishing to satisfy the crowd, Pilate released Barabbas for them, and after having Jesus scourged, he handed Him over to be crucified. The soldiers took Him away into the palace (that is, the Praetorium), and they called together the whole Roman cohort. They dressed Him up in purple, and after twisting a crown of thorns, they put it on Him; and they began to acclaim Him, 'Hail, King of the Jews!' They kept beating His head with a reed, and spitting on Him, and kneeling and bowing before Him. After they had mocked Him, they took the purple robe off Him and put His own garments on Him. And they led Him out to crucify Him. [...] Then they brought Him to the place Golgotha, which is translated, Place of a Skull. They tried to give Him wine mixed with myrrh; but He did not take it. And they crucified Him..." (Mark 15:15-24).

After being born into this world and living a relatively short life here, Jesus died. However, more than anyone else,

His death was significant. The *day of Jesus' crucifixion* was the day in which He died on the cross for our sins. As we have already seen, this was part of God's plan from the beginning (Revelation 13:8).

The Background

Jesus lived a perfect life – In the previous lesson, we highlighted Jesus' humanity – the fact that He came to earth and *"partook"* of *"flesh and blood"* and was *"made like His brethren in all things"* (Hebrews 2:14, 17). However, there was a significant difference between the life of Jesus and the lives of others. Paul described the universal problem of sin: *"For all have sinned and fall short of the glory of God"* (Romans 3:23). In contrast, Jesus was *"separated from sinners"* (Hebrews 7:26) because He was perfectly sinless.

> *"For you have been called for this purpose, since Christ also suffered for you, leaving you an example for you to follow in His steps, who committed no sin, nor was any deceit found in His mouth"* (1 Peter 2:21-22).

Jesus' life is an example for us to follow. But more than that, the fact that Jesus was sinless meant that His crucifixion was wholly undeserved. In Isaiah's prophecy of the suffering of Christ, he said, *"His grave was assigned with wicked men, yet He was with a rich man in His death, because He had done no violence, nor was there any deceit in His mouth"* (Isaiah 53:9). When Pilate examined Jesus, he recognized that there was *"no guilt in Him"* (John 19:4); but he caved to the pressure of the Jews and allowed Jesus to be put to death anyway.

Jesus was rejected by His people – Again, this was prophesied by Isaiah: *"He was despised and forsaken of men, a man of sorrows and acquainted with grief; and like one from whom men hide their face He was despised, and we did not esteem Him"* (Isaiah 53:3). When Pilate presented Jesus before the Jews as their *"King,"* the people called for His crucifixion, even going so far as to willingly claim Caesar as their king (John 19:4-5).

The Jews rejected Jesus despite what the Scriptures said about Him. Paul wrote, *"Therefore the Law has become our tutor to lead us to Christ, so that we may be justified by faith"* (Galatians 3:24). Jesus said that the Scriptures testified about Him (John 5:39); and He explained later that *"all things which* [were] *written about* [Him] *in the Law of Moses and the Prophets and the Psalms must be fulfilled"* (Luke 24:44). Yet despite this evidence from the Scriptures which were *"read in the synagogues every Sabbath"* (Acts 15:21), the Jews rejected Him.

They also rejected Jesus despite what they saw Jesus say and do. In addition to the witness of the Scriptures (John 5:39), Jesus said that His works testified of Him (John 5:36). When the Jews demanded Jesus to *"tell* [them] *plainly"* if He was the Christ, He said, *"I told you, and you do not believe; the works that I do in My Father's name, these testify of Me"* (John 10:24-25). There was ample evidence to show that Jesus was the Christ, the Son of God; yet the people ignored this evidence and rejected Him.

Jesus knew all that was going to happen to Him – When Jesus was led away to be crucified, it did not come as a surprise to Him. Earlier in the evening before His arrest, He knew *"that His hour had come that He would depart out of this world to the Father"* (John 13:1). When Judas came with the mob to the Garden, Jesus already knew *"all the things that were coming upon Him"* (John 18:4).

With all of the prophecies that pointed to His death on the cross (Isaiah 53:3-9; Psalm 22; *et al.*), it should not be surprising that Jesus knew what was going to happen. After all, He was the Word in the flesh (John 1:1, 14).

Even while He was on the earth, Jesus indicated that He knew what was to transpire and provided clues to others about what would happen. He told Nicodemus, *"As Moses lifted up the serpent in the wilderness, even so must the Son of Man be lifted up"* (John 3:14). Later He told His disciples, *"And I, if I am lifted up from the earth, will draw all men to Myself"* (John 12:32). John added that this statement was made *"to indicate the kind of death by which He was to die"* (John 12:33). Matthew recorded, *"From that time Jesus began to show His disciples that He must go to Jerusalem, and suffer many things from the elders and chief priests and scribes, and be killed, and be raised up on the third day"* (Matthew 16:21). None of these things caught Jesus by surprise. He knew what was going to take place and came to do the Father's will (Hebrews 10:5-10).

The Events on That Day

Jesus' prayer in the Garden – In His prayer, Jesus demonstrated a willingness to submit to the Father, regardless of what the outcome would be: *"Abba! Father! All things are possible for You; remove this cup from Me; yet not what I will, but what You will"* (Mark 14:36). Paul used this example to make the point that we must be willing to humble ourselves as Jesus did: *"He humbled Himself by becoming obedient to the point of death, even death on a cross"* (Philippians 2:8).

However, it is important to understand that Jesus did not grudgingly go along with the Father's will. When He prayed for the *"cup"* to be removed (Mark 14:36), He was not expressing a desire to avoid the cross. As we have already noticed, Jesus knew what was going to take place as far as His death on the cross. Despite this, He clearly articulated His willingness to suffer this: *"For this reason the Father loves Me, because I lay down My life so that I may take it again. No one has taken it away from Me, but I lay it down on My own initiative. I have authority to lay it down, and I have authority to take it up again. This commandment I received from My Father"* (John 10:17-18). Jesus prayed "that if it were possible, the hour might pass Him by" (Mark 14:35). In other words, He was not praying that He might not have to endure the crucifixion; He was praying that the events of this *"hour"* might be accomplished. His prayer was not to *escape* the cross, but to be delivered *through* the cross.

Jesus' trial and condemnation – There were several stages to the trial of Jesus. He was first tried by the priests and faced false accusations, insults, and physical abuse (Mark 14:53-65). He then stood before Pilate where He was questioned and, though He was found to be innocent, was condemned to death (Mark 15:2-5, 10-15). Luke also recorded the fact that Jesus was sent by Pilate to Herod where He was treated with contempt and mocked before being sent back to Pilate (Luke 23:11). Jesus endured all of these things leading up to His crucifixion.

Jesus' suffering and death on the cross – Before the cross, Jesus was scourged when Pilate yielded to the Jews' demands to have Jesus crucified (Mark 15:15). After this happened, the soldiers mocked and abused Him before taking Him to the place where He would be crucified: *"The soldiers took Him away* *into the palace (that is, the Praetorium), and they called together the whole Roman cohort. They dressed Him up in purple, and after twisting a crown of thorns, they put it on Him; and they began to acclaim Him, 'Hail, King of the Jews!' They kept beating His head with a reed, and spitting on Him, and kneeling and bowing before Him. After they mocked Him, they took the purple robe off Him and put His own garments on Him. And they led Him out to crucify Him"* (Mark 15:16-20).

When Jesus was crucified, His hands and feet were nailed to the cross (Psalm 22:16; John 20:25). Once He was hung in the air, the mocking continued (Mark 15:29-33). The physical abuse and torture His body endured throughout the ordeal were extreme. In describing in detail the suffering endured by those condemned to this punishment, Henry E. Dosker wrote, "The victim of crucifixion literally died a thousand deaths" (International Standard Bible Encyclopedia). Again, Jesus knew *"all the things that were coming upon Him"* (John 18:4); and He went to the cross anyway.

Signs in His death – There were several signs that accompanied Jesus' death on the cross:

- Darkness from the sixth to ninth hour – *"When the sixth hour came, darkness fell over the whole land until the ninth hour"* (Mark 15:33).
- The veil of the temple was torn – *"And Jesus uttered a loud cry, and breathed His last. And the veil of the temple was torn in two from top to bottom"* (Mark 15:37-38).
- The earth shook, tombs were opened, and the dead were raised – *"The tombs were opened, and many bodies of the saints who had fallen asleep*

> *were raised; and coming out of the tombs after His resurrection they entered the holy city and appeared to many"* (Matthew 27:52-53).

All of these things led the centurion to conclude, *"Truly this man was the Son of God"* (Mark 15:39).

Key Lessons

The need for a sacrifice – In discussing the comparison between the sacrifices offered under the Law of Moses and the sacrifice of Christ, the Hebrew writer said, *"And according to the Law, one may almost say, all things are cleansed with blood, and without shedding of blood there is no forgiveness"* (Hebrews 9:22). Animal sacrifices had been offered *"continually year by year,"* but the system under the old law contained *"only a shadow of the good things to come and not the very form of things"* (Hebrews 10:1). Because of this, the Hebrew writer said, *"For it is impossible for the blood of bulls and goats to take away sins"* (Hebrews 10:4).

Since the animal sacrifices offered under the Law of Moses would not take away sins (Hebrews 10:4) and there could be no forgiveness without blood being shed (Hebrews 9:22), another sacrifice was necessary. In order for forgiveness to be possible, Jesus would have to shed His blood on the cross. The Hebrew writer explained, *"Therefore, when He comes into the world, He says, 'Sacrifice and offering You have not desired, but a body You have prepared for Me... By this will we have been sanctified through the offering of the body of Jesus Christ once for all"* (Hebrews 10:5, 10). The *"blood of Christ"* is able to *"cleanse* [our] *conscience from dead works to serve the living God"* (Hebrews 9:14).

We remember this sacrifice when we observe the Lord's Supper. Before His death, Jesus instituted the Lord's Supper and gave the cup as a symbol of His *"blood of the covenant, which is poured out for many for forgiveness of sins"* (Matthew 26:28). This memorial is to be observed each first day of the week (cf. Acts 20:7) because of how important it is for us to remember. Paul told the Corinthians, *"For as often as you eat this bread and drink the cup, you proclaim the Lord's death until He comes"* (1 Corinthians 11:26). We must continue to remember and proclaim Christ's death even today.

Jesus' qualifications – Paul told Timothy, *"For there is one God, and one mediator also between God and men, the man Christ Jesus"* (1 Timothy 2:5). He was qualified to serve as mediator because He shared characteristics of both parties. *"The fullness of Deity* [dwelt] *in bodily form"* in Him (Colossians 2:9). He also *"became flesh, and dwelt among us"* (John 1:14). Therefore, He was able to be the mediator – "a go-between" (Vine's) – between God and men. He was able to bring about reconciliation between both parties (Romans 5:10).

Jesus was different from every high priest in that He was perfectly qualified. Notice what the Hebrew writer said: *"For it was fitting for us to have such a high priest, holy, innocent, undefiled, separated from sinners and exalted above the heavens; who does not need daily, like those high priests, to offer up sacrifices, first for His own sins and then for the sins of the people, because this He did once for all when He offered up Himself. For the Law appoints men as high priests who are weak, but the word of the oath, which came after the Law, appoints a Son, made perfect forever"* (Hebrews 7:26-28). No one else would have ever been qualified to fulfill this role.

Furthermore, only Jesus was qualified to *offer* and to *be* the sacrifice for our sins. Notice in the passage above that the priests under the Law of Moses would *"offer up sacrifices"* of bulls and goats while Jesus made a perfect sacrifice *"once for all when He offered up Himself"* (Hebrews 7:27).

The effectiveness of Jesus' sacrifice – Unlike the sacrifices that were offered under the Law of Moses, Jesus' sacrifice was perfectly able to take away sins. Again, the sacrifices under the old law that were offered *"continually"* could never *"take away sins"* (Hebrews 10:1, 4). Yet Jesus' sacrifice was just *"one offering"* that *"perfected for all time those who are sanctified"* (Hebrews 10:14). John wrote, *"The blood of Jesus... cleanses us from all sin"* (1 John 1:7).

The effectiveness of Jesus' sacrifice on the cross was for *everyone*. Jesus said, *"For God so loved the world, that He gave His only begotten Son, that whoever believes in Him shall not perish, but have eternal life"* (John 3:16). This is different from what is taught in the Calvinist doctrine of "limited atonement" – the idea that Jesus did not die for the *world*, but only for the *elect*. Yet Paul wrote, *"For the grace of God has appeared, bringing salvation to all men"* (Titus 2:11). The salvation that was made possible by Jesus' sacrifice on the cross is open to everyone.

However, this salvation is conditional. Though God's grace has *"appeared...to all men"* (Titus 2:11), we know that not all will be saved (Matthew 7:13-14). How can this be? The only way to harmonize these passages is by concluding that God offers salvation to everyone but will only save those who meet His conditions. Jesus said, *"He who has believed and has been baptized shall be saved; but he who has disbelieved shall be condemned"* (Mark 16:16). He is *"to all those who obey Him the source of eternal salvation"* (Hebrews 5:9). Jesus' crucifixion has made salvation available, but we must take advantage of this offer.

Conclusion

In the previous lesson, we highlighted God's love as one of the key lessons regarding Jesus' birth. However, the death of Christ on the cross was necessarily connected to this as well. Because God loved the world, He sent Jesus into the world to die on the cross for us.

> *"But God demonstrates His own love toward us, in that while we were yet sinners, Christ died for us"* (Romans 5:8).

Salvation is open to all, but we need to take advantage of His offer of salvation. Since He gave His life for us, we need to give our lives to Him and offer ourselves as *"a living and holy sacrifice, acceptable to God"* (Romans 12:1).

Questions for Discussion and Reflection

1. What kind of life had Jesus lived leading up to His crucifixion?

2. Was Jesus surprised by His arrest and crucifixion? How do we know?

3. What was Jesus' prayer prior to His arrest?

4. Why did Jesus need to die on the cross?

5. Who stands to benefit from Jesus' death on the cross?

3/31/21

4

THE DAY OF JESUS' RESURRECTION

> *"For I delivered to you as of first importance what I also received, that Christ died for our sins according to the Scriptures, and that He was buried, and that He was raised on the third day according to the Scriptures"* (1 Corinthians 15:3-4).

On the third day after Jesus' crucifixion, an event occurred that was *"of first importance"* (1 Corinthians 15:3) – the *day of Jesus' resurrection*. Without Jesus being raised from the dead, our *"faith is worthless"* (1 Corinthians 15:17); but since He was raised from the dead, we have hope (1 Corinthians 15:20-23).

The Background

Jesus was buried – After Jesus was crucified, Joseph of Arimathea went to Pilate to ask for the body of Jesus in order to bury Him. Pilate granted him permission, so *"Joseph took the body and wrapped it in a clean linen cloth, and laid it in his own new tomb, which he had hewn out in the rock; and he rolled a large stone against the entrance of the tomb and went away"* (Matthew

27:59-60).

There are many who want to deny the resurrection of Jesus and will claim that Jesus was not *really* dead after His crucifixion. However, Jesus did not just *appear* to be dead; He was truly dead. The soldiers who crucified Jesus – certainly not ones who would plot together with Jesus and the disciples to stage His death – were able to see for themselves *"that He was already dead"* (John 19:33). This was why they did not break His legs like they did with the two thieves (John 19:31-32). There was no need to do this since Jesus was already dead. To confirm that He was really dead, John recorded, *"One of the soldiers pierced His side with a spear, and immediately blood and water came out"* (John 19:34).

Even one of Jesus' disciples – Joseph of Arimathea – prepared His body for burial and left Him in a sealed tomb. He did not see signs of life while preparing His body. When he put Jesus' body in the tomb, he sealed the tomb and left. Despite the fact that Joseph was a disciple, it seems as though he had no expectation that Jesus would be raised; so he prepared His body for an actual burial.

The tomb was guarded – The chief priests and Pharisees were determined to prevent anything from happening to the body of Jesus. So they asked Pilate to make the grave secure and explained the reason for their request: *"Sir, we remember that when He was still alive that deceiver said, 'After three days I am to rise again.' Therefore, give orders for the grave to be made secure until the third day, otherwise His disciples may come and steal Him away and say to the people, 'He has risen from the dead,' and the last deception will be worse than the first'"* (Matthew 27:63-64).

The Jewish leaders were concerned that Jesus' disciples would remove the body, then claim that He was alive. With the following that Jesus was able to gain before His death, they knew this would lead even more people to believe in Him. So Pilate said, *"You have a guard; go, make it as secure as you know how"* (Matthew 27:65). They certainly would have done this because they did not want there to be any credibility to reports that Jesus might be alive. They wanted to be able to show that the tomb was still sealed (Matthew 27:66).

The disciples were in fear – After Jesus' resurrection, John recorded, *"So when it was evening on that day, the first day of the week, and when the doors were shut where the disciples were, for fear of the Jews, Jesus came and stood in their midst and said to them, 'Peace be with you'"* (John 20:19). Before Jesus appeared to them, these men were afraid. After Jesus was killed, they surely thought they could be too. Just a few days before this, Jesus warned them, *"Remember the word that I said to you, 'A slave is not greater than his master.' If they persecuted Me, they will also persecute you..."* (John 15:20). They had every reason to believe that they were going to be targeted next.

Interestingly, this was after the first report that Jesus had been raised. Mary Magdalene told the disciples, *"I have seen the Lord"* (John 20:18). However, at first, the disciples were skeptical and *"would not believe"* this report (Luke 24:11). Yet even if they did believe Mary's report – or even if they just wanted to believe it – there was still uncertainty about what was to happen next. Even with Jesus being raised from the dead, they still did not know what troubles and persecution they were going to face in the near future.

The Events on That Day

The tomb was found empty – *"Now after the Sabbath, as it began to dawn toward the first day of the week, Mary Magdalene and the other Mary came to look at the grave"* (Matthew 28:1). However, when these women arrived, they saw that the stone had been rolled away and that Jesus' body was gone. Instead of finding Jesus, they were greeted by angels who announced that He had risen: *"The angel said to the women, 'Do not be afraid; for I know that you are looking for Jesus who has been crucified. He is not here, for He has risen, just as He said. Come, see the place where He was lying'"* (Matthew 28:5-6). These women were able to see for themselves that the body of Jesus was not in the tomb.

It is important to note that the ones who came were not expecting to find the tomb empty. On the way, the women *"were saying to one another, 'Who will roll away the stone for us from the entrance of the tomb?'"* (Mark 16:3). When they reported to Jesus' disciples what they found, their *"words appeared to them as nonsense, and they would not believe them"* (Luke 24:11). This is significant because of the false story that would be spread by Jesus' enemies to try to explain away the empty tomb – that the disciples stole the body (Matthew 28:13). Not only did the disciples not steal the body, they also expected the body of Jesus to still be on the tomb when they heard this report. When they would finally see Jesus, it would cause them to have to change their minds about what had happened.

Jesus began appearing to His disciples – He initially appeared to the women who came to the tomb (Matthew 28:9). According to Mark's account, Mary Magdalene was the first of these women to see Jesus alive from the dead (Mark 16:9). He appeared to two disciples on the road to Emmaus (Luke 24:13-31), then to the rest of the disciples (Luke 24:36-43). In his letter to Corinth, Paul listed many of the ones who were eyewitnesses of Jesus after His resurrection:

> *"And that He was buried, and that He was raised on the third day according to the Scriptures, and that He appeared to Cephas, then to the twelve. After that He appeared to more than five hundred brethren at one time, most of whom remain until now, but some have fallen asleep; then He appeared to James, then to all the apostles; and last of all, as to one untimely born, He appeared to me also"* (1 Corinthians 15:4-8).

All in all, Jesus appeared on several different occasions to *hundreds* of individuals to show that He had in fact been raised from the dead.

Jesus' enemies tried to explain away the empty tomb – As we already noticed, the chief priests and Pharisees were worried about Jesus' disciples stealing His body and claiming that He had risen from the dead; so they requested and received a guard to secure the tomb as best they could (Matthew 27:62-66). However, this did not prevent Jesus from being raised from the dead and departing from the tomb. So they had to come up with another explanation for what happened.

> *"Now while they were on their way, some of the guard came into the city and reported to the chief priests all that had happened. And when they had assembled with the elders and consulted together,*

> *they gave a large sum of money to the soldiers, and said, 'You are to say, "His disciples came by night and stole Him away while we were asleep." And if this should come to the governor's ears, we will win him over and keep you out of trouble.' And they took the money and did as they had been instructed; and this story was widely spread among the Jews, and is to this day"* (Matthew 28:11-15).

There were some obvious holes in their story. Perhaps the most notable was this: if they were *asleep,* how would they know Jesus' disciples came and took the body? However, the fact that this story was illogical did not prevent it from spreading. People will often believe what they want to believe (cf. 2 Timothy 4:3-4), even if it is not in harmony with truth and reason.

Key Lessons

Jesus' power over death – As we noticed in the lesson about the day of Jesus' birth, He came into this world in the form of man (Hebrews 2:14; Philippians 2:5-8; Colossians 2:9). One of the reasons for this was so He could destroy Satan's power over death.

> *"Therefore, since the children share in flesh and blood, He Himself likewise also partook of the same, that through death He might render powerless him who had the power of death, that is, the devil, and might free those who through fear of death were subject to slavery all their lives"* (Hebrews 2:14-15).

Others had been raised from the dead prior to Jesus' resurrection. In the Old Testament, Elijah raised a widow's son (1 Kings 17:21-22), Elisha raised the Shunammite's son (2 Kings 4:32-35), and a man was raised when his body touched the bones of Elisha's dead body (2 Kings 13:20-21). During the ministry of Jesus, He raised the widow's son in Nain (Luke 7:11-15), Jairus' daughter (Luke 8:52-55), and Lazarus (John 11:43-44). When He was crucified, there were dead saints who were raised (Matthew 27:52). However, Jesus was the first to be *"raised from the dead... never to die again"* (Romans 6:9).

Hope for the resurrection – Those who had been raised from the dead prior to Jesus' resurrection did die again. But through Jesus, we have hope for a resurrection like His. However, this hope is only for those who will obey Him. Notice what Paul wrote:

> *"Therefore we have been buried with Him through baptism into death, so that as Christ was raised from the dead through the glory of the Father, so we too might walk in newness of life. For if we have become united with Him in the likeness of His death, certainly we shall also be in the likeness of His resurrection, knowing this, that our old self was crucified with Him, in order that our body of sin might be done away with, so that we would no longer be slaves to sin; for he who has died is freed from sin. Now if we have died with Christ, we believe that we shall also live with Him"* (Romans 6:4-8).

If we will die to sin, be buried with Christ in baptism, and walk in newness of life, we can also be raised *"never to die again"* (Romans 6:9). Jesus is *"the resurrection and the life"* (John 11:25). Even though we may die, we will receive the reward if we are faithful to Him. Those who have *"fallen asleep in Jesus"* will receive the same reward as those who are *"alive and remain"* when the Lord returns (1 Thessalonians 4:14-17).

Therefore, we do not need to fear death. In writing of the hope of the resurrection, Paul told the Corinthians, *"The last enemy that will be abolished is death"* (1 Corinthians 15:26). Regarding this event, Paul wrote, *"But when this perishable will have put on the imperishable, and this mortal will have put on immortality, then will come about the saying that is written, 'Death is swallowed up in victory. O death, where is your victory? O death, where is your sting? The sting of death is sin, and the power of sin is the law; but thanks be to God, who gives us the victory through our Lord Jesus Christ"* (1 Corinthians 15:54-57).

Even if we face persecution for the cause of Christ, we can have confidence in the hope of the resurrection. Jesus said, *"Do not fear those who kill the body but are unable to kill the soul; but rather fear Him who is able to destroy both soul and body in hell"* (Matthew 10:28). We may be *"considered as sheep to be slaughtered,"* yet we *"overwhelmingly conquer through Him who loved us"* (Romans 8:36-37).

Evidence for our faith – God does not expect us to take a "leap of faith," but to believe based upon the evidence He has given us. *"Now faith is the substance of things hoped for, the evidence of things not seen"* (Hebrews 11:1, KJV).

When it comes to having faith in the fact that Jesus was raised from the dead, we have evidence upon which to base our faith. There were *hundreds* of eyewitnesses who saw Jesus alive after His crucifixion (1 Corinthians 15:5-8). Not only did these individuals provide testimony, they affirmed their believe in the resurrection despite being persecuted for it (Acts 4:18-20; 5:27-29, 40-42; 7:54-8:4; *et al.*). The only reason why they would do this was because they *knew* that Jesus' resurrection was a fact and they *knew* this gave them hope.

Yet this was more than just evidence that God could raise someone from the dead. Paul wrote, "*Who was declared the Son of God with power by the resurrection from the dead, according to the Spirit of holiness, Jesus Christ our Lord*" (Romans 1:4). Jesus' resurrection proved He was the Son of God and verified all of His claims to that effect.

Conclusion

Jesus died on the cross in order to make salvation possible for us. However, His sacrifice would have been ineffective without the resurrection. His resurrection gives us hope. If we will conform to His death, burial, and resurrection and then walk in newness of life, we can be "*united with Him...in the likeness of His resurrection*" (Romans 6:3-5).

Questions for Discussion and Reflection

1. How do we know that Jesus was really dead prior to His resurrection?

2. What was the emotional state of Jesus' apostles before His resurrection?

3. How many people were eye-witnesses of Jesus being alive after His crucifixion?

4. Why does Jesus' resurrection give us hope?

5. What evidence is there to show that Jesus did rise from the dead?

5

THE DAY OF PENTECOST

> *"When the day of Pentecost had come, they were all together in one place. And suddenly there came from heaven a noise like a violent rushing wind, and it filled the whole house where they were sitting. And there appeared to them tongues as of fire distributing themselves, and they rested on each of them. And they were all filled with the Holy Spirit and began to speak with other tongues, as the Spirit was giving them utterance"* (Acts 2:1-4).

The day of Pentecost – called the Feast of Weeks in the Old Testament (Exodus 34:22; Deuteronomy 16:10) – occurred fifty days after the Passover (Leviticus 23:15-16). This was to be observed every year by the Jews; however, this lesson is not about the annual event, but one specific day – the *day of Pentecost* following Jesus' ascension.

The Background

Jesus spoke about the kingdom – As we noticed in the previous lesson, Jesus appeared to His disciples on several different occasions following His resurrection (Matthew 28:9; Luke 24:13-31, 36-43; 1 Corinthians 15:4-8). However, He spent more time with those whom He had chosen to be His apostles. Luke emphasized this in the opening statement of the book of Acts:

> *"The first account I composed, Theophilus, about all that Jesus began to do and teach, until the day when He was taken up to heaven, after He had by the Holy Spirit given orders to the apostles whom He had chosen. To these He also presented Himself alive after His suffering, by many convincing proofs, appearing to them over a period of forty days and speaking of the things concerning the kingdom of God"* (Acts 1:1-3).

For forty days, Jesus spent time with these men and spoke to them about things pertaining to the kingdom. While it is doubtful that this was all that He discussed with them, we can safely conclude from Luke's account that this must have been the *primary* theme of Jesus' discussions with the apostles during this time. This is significant, especially as we will notice what took place on this day.

Jesus told His apostles they would be His witnesses – Jesus said to them, *"But you will receive power when the Holy Spirit has come upon you; and you shall be My witnesses both in Jerusalem, and in all Judea and Samaria, and even to the remotest part of the earth"* (Acts 1:8). He had already told them that they would *"testify"* about Him since they had *"been with* [Him] *from the beginning"* (John 15:27).

The apostles' being *"witnesses"* to Jesus would be done in Jerusalem, Judea, Samaria, and throughout the world – a reference to their work in carrying out the Great Commission. This was recorded expressly in the synoptic gospels with each one emphasizing different details. Matthew emphasized the apostles' work in *making disciples* (Matthew 28:19-20). Mark focused on their role in *preaching the gospel* (Mark 16:15-16). Luke stressed the fact that the apostles would *testify* of Christ as His witnesses:

> *"And He said to them, 'Thus it is written, that the Christ would suffer and rise again from the dead the third day, and that repentance for forgiveness of sins would be proclaimed in His name to all the nations, beginning from Jerusalem. You are witnesses of these things. And behold, I am sending forth the promise of My Father upon you; but you are to stay in the city until you are clothed with power from on high"* (Luke 24:46-49).

When the apostles spoke about the risen Lord, beginning at the day of Pentecost, they would do so as *eye-witnesses* (cf. 1 John 1:1-3).

Jesus ascended to heaven – After Jesus told His apostles they would be His witnesses (Acts 1:8), *"He was lifted up while they were looking on, and a cloud received Him out of their sight"* (Acts 1:9). However, when this happened, these men were not left to wonder about when or how He might return; two angels explained this to them: *"Men of Galilee, why do you* *stand looking into the sky? This Jesus, who has been taken up from you into heaven, will come in just the same way as you have watched Him go into heaven"* (Acts 1:11). This would be done just as Jesus said it would happen (John 14:3).

The Events on That Day

The Holy Spirit came upon the apostles – This was how the events on the day of Pentecost had to begin:

> *"When the day of Pentecost had come, they were all together in one place. And suddenly there came from heaven a noise like a violent rushing wind, and it filled the whole house where they were sitting. And there appeared to them tongues as of fire distributing themselves, and they rested on each one of them. And they were all filled with the Holy Spirit and began to speak with other tongues, as the Spirit was giving them utterance"* (Acts 2:1-4).

The coming of the Holy Spirit upon the apostles was a fulfillment of prophecy. We already noticed that Jesus told His apostles, *"You will receive power when the Holy Spirit has come upon you"* (Acts 1:8). Just before that, He said, *"John baptized with water, but you will be baptized with the Holy Spirit not many days from now"* (Acts 1:5). But long before this, the prophet Joel foretold this event: *"It will come about after this that I will pour out My Spirit on all mankind; and your sons and daughters will prophesy, your old men will dream dreams, your young men will see visions. [...] And it will come about that whoever calls on the name of the Lord will be delivered"* (Joel 2:28-32). Peter cited this prophecy in his sermon on that day. While some people were amazed or confused and others were mocking what was taking place, Peter explained, *"This is what was spoken of through the prophet Joel"* (Acts 2:16-21).

The reason why the Holy Spirit came upon the apostles was to help them complete their mission – to carry out the Great Commission as witnesses of Jesus (Luke 24:46-49; Acts 1:8). Shortly before His death, Jesus promised to send the Holy Spirit to them for this reason:

> *"But the Helper, the Holy Spirit, whom the Father will send in My name, He will teach you all things, and bring to your remembrance all that I said to you"* (John 14:26).
>
> *"When the Helper comes, whom I will send to you from the Father, that is the Spirit of truth who proceeds from the Father, He will testify about Me, and you will testify also, because you have been with Me from the beginning"* (John 15:26-27).
>
> *"But when He, the Spirit of truth, comes, He will guide you into all truth; for He will not speak on His own initiative, but whatever He hears, He will speak; and He will disclose to you what is to come"* (John 16:13).

As the apostles were commissioned to preach the gospel (Mark 16:15), make disciples (Matthew 28:19), and testify of Christ (Luke 24:46-48), the Holy Spirit came upon them on the day of Pentecost so they could begin this work.

Peter preached the first gospel sermon – For the sake of space, the entire text of Peter's sermon will not be included here (Acts 2:14-40); but the thrust of the message can be seen in the verses below:

> *"Men of Israel, listen to these words: Jesus the Nazarene, a man attested to you by God with miracles and wonders and signs which God performed through Him in your midst, just as you yourselves know—this Man, delivered over by the predetermined plan and foreknowledge of God, you nailed to a cross by the hands of godless men and put Him to death. But God raised Him up again, putting an end to the agony of death, since it was impossible for Him to be held in its power"* (Acts 2:22-24).

Peter cited various prophecies to show that Jesus' death and resurrection were part of God's plan – His soul would not remain in Hades (Acts 2:25-28; cf. Psalm 16:8-11), He would be a descendant of David and sit on his throne (Acts 2:30; cf. Psalm 132:11; 2 Samuel 7:12), and He would sit at the right hand of God until His enemies became His footstool (Acts 2:34-35; cf. Psalm 110:1). Not only did Peter show that Jesus' death and resurrection were part of God's plan, he also showed that God revealed through the prophets that this would happen.

While Peter's sermon on the day of Pentecost is often referred to as the "first gospel sermon," there is a sense in which the gospel was preached before this. Paul wrote that *"the gospel"* had been *"preached...beforehand to Abraham"* (Galatians 3:8). Both John the Baptist and Jesus Himself preached the gospel (Luke 3:18; Matthew 4:23). However, when the gospel was preached before Pentecost, it was preached *in promise*. On the day of Pentecost, it was preached for the first time *in fact*. Jesus had been crucified and raised from the dead – facts that were *"of first importance"* to the message of the gospel (1 Corinthians 15:1-4).

When Peter preached on the day of Pentecost, three thousand people responded: *"So then, those who had received his word were baptized; and that day there were added about three thousand souls"* (Acts 2:41). What did it mean to receive his word? Notice what Luke recorded:

> *"Now when they heard this, they were pierced to the heart, and said to Peter and the rest of the apostles, 'Brethren, what shall we do?' Peter said to them, 'Repent, and each of you be baptized in the name of Jesus Christ for the forgiveness of your sins; and you will receive the gift of the Holy Spirit'"* (Acts 2:37-38).

The ones who *"received his word"* (Acts 2:41) were those who did what Peter told them to do. They believed, repented, and were baptized for the remission of sins.

The Lord's church was established – From the day of Pentecost onward, God *"added to the church daily such as should be saved"* (Acts 2:47, KJV). The church was active in Jerusalem in assembling together (Acts 2:42), helping one another (Acts 2:44-45), spending time together (Acts 2:46), and praising God (Acts 2:47). These individuals were not merely recorded on a list of members, they were actively involved in the church.

It is also important to note that this was also the establishment of the Lord's kingdom. When Jesus promised to *"build* [His] *church,"* He told Peter He would *"give* [him] *the keys of the kingdom"* (Matthew 16:18-19). He was not referring to two different institutions; rather, the *church* was the *kingdom*. Jesus told His disciples that *"the kingdom"* would *"come with power"* (Mark 9:1). They would *"receive* [this] *power when the Holy Spirit* [had] *come upon* [them]" (Acts 1:8). This Spirit came upon them on *"the day of Pentecost"* (Acts 2:1-4), when the church was established.

Jesus promised to *"build* [His] *church"* (Matthew 16:18); and this *"kingdom"* would *"never be destroyed"* (Daniel 2:44).

Key Lessons

The Lord's church is open to all – Though the gospel was first preached to the Jews on the day of Pentecost, it would eventually be taken to other nations. Peter alluded to this in his sermon: *"For the promise is for you and your children and for all who are far off, as many as the Lord our God will call to Himself"* (Acts 2:39). This was also prophesied by Isaiah: *"Now it will come about that in the last days the mountain of the house of the Lord will be established as the chief of the mountains, and will be raised above the hills; and all the nations will stream to it"* (Isaiah 2:2). The Lord's church, which was established on the day of Pentecost, would be open to all.

The Lord's plan was for the apostles to *"go into all the world and preach the gospel to all creation"* (Mark 16:15). Paul explained to the brethren in Thessalonica that the gospel is the means by which God calls us (2 Thessalonians 2:14). Since this call was intended for and has been extended to all, we can safely conclude that God will welcome all who will come to Him. However, we do not merely need to conclude that; Peter explained that specifically when he spoke to the household of

Cornelius: *"I most certainly understand now that God is not one to show partiality, but in every nation the man who fears Him and does what is right is welcome to Him"* (Acts 10:34-35).

God welcomes all from every nation into just *"one body"* (Ephesians 4:4). Both Jews and Gentiles have been reconciled *"in one body to God"* (Ephesians 2:16) – this body being the church (Ephesians 1:22-23) which began on the day of Pentecost.

God adds people to the church – Luke clearly recorded, *"The Lord added to the church daily such as should be saved"* (Acts 2:47, KJV). The ones that God added were those who believed, repented, and were baptized (Acts 2:37-38).

Since God adds people to the church, that means that we do not get to dictate the terms of admission to Him. We can be guilty of doing this in two ways:

1. We might accept people as members of the church whom God has not added – Some time after Paul obeyed the gospel in Damascus, he returned to Jerusalem and *"was trying to associate with the disciples; but they were all afraid of him, not believing that he was a disciple"* (Acts 9:26). At first, the brethren in the church in Jerusalem had no reason to believe that Saul was a disciple. Until they knew he had been converted (and, therefore, added by God to the church), they could not accept him into their fellowship (cf. Ephesians 5:11; 2 Corinthians 6:14-17). Yet many are tempted to accept

anyone and everyone, regardless of whether they are truly the Lord's disciples.

2. We might refuse to accept those whom God has added to the church – After the gospel began being preached to Gentiles (Acts 10:34-48; 11:1-18; 14:27; 15:3), some Jewish Christians started to insist that these brethren had to be *"circumcised according to the custom of Moses"* in order to *"be saved"* (Acts 15:1). Of course, the Lord never required this. Peter said, *"Now therefore why do you put God to the test by placing upon the neck of the disciples a yoke which neither our fathers nor we have been able to bear? But we believe that we are saved through the grace of the Lord Jesus, in the same way as they also are"* (Acts 15:10-11). Yet some people are like these Judaizing teachers and want to add more requirements than the Lord gave for us to be added to the church.

We simply need to be preaching God's plan of salvation – the gospel which Peter preached on the day of Pentecost – so that others can hear what they need to do to be saved and be encouraged to make their lives right with Him through faithful obedience.

Responsibilities for those in the church – It is not enough for us to simply be *"added to the church"* (Acts 2:47, KJV). There are certain things that the Lord expects us to do after we are part of His church. Notice what Luke recorded about the early church immediately after Peter preached the first gospel sermon:

- *"They were continually devoting themselves to the apostles' teaching and to fellowship, to the breaking of bread and to prayer"* (Acts 2:42). They were worshiping God as He had prescribed. This harmonizes with the statement Jesus made about the fact that we *"must worship in spirit and truth"* (John 4:24).
- *"And all those who had believed were together and had all things in common; and they began selling their property and possessions and were sharing them with all, as anyone might have need"* (Acts 2:44-45). They were willing to help others, just as we need to be. John wrote, *"Beloved, if God so loved us, we also ought to love one another"* (1 John 4:11).
- *"Day by day continuing with one mind in the temple"* (Acts 2:46). They were united in one mind. This unity was based upon their continuing in *"the apostles' teaching"* (Acts 2:42). This was the *"unity of the Spirit"* that Paul described (Ephesians 4:3). We must have agreement and harmony with one another based upon what the apostles taught. Jesus prayed for this: *"I do not ask on behalf of these alone, but for those also who believe in Me through their word; that they may all be one; even as You, Father, are in Me and I in You, that they also may be in Us, so that the world may believe that You sent Me"* (John 17:20-21). Therefore, it must be a priority for us as well.
- *"Breaking bread from house to house, they were taking their meals together with gladness and sincerity of heart"* (Acts 2:46). They were

regularly together with other Christians. This is important for us so that we can *"encourage one another day after day...so that none of you will be hardened by the deceitfulness of sin"* (Hebrews 3:13).

As members of the Lord's church, we are not to be idle, nor are we to do whatever seems right to us. We simply need to carry out the Lord's will as He has revealed it to us in His word.

Conclusion

The Lord's church was established on the day of Pentecost. This was the beginning of a kingdom that would never be destroyed. This kingdom is open to all. We can be part of it by doing what the Lord has said we must do to be saved (Acts 2:37-38).

Questions for Discussion and Reflection

1. What is significant about the fact that the apostles were eye-witnesses of Jesus?

2. When the Holy Spirit came upon the apostles, what role did He come to fulfill?

3. How did the ones who received Peter's message respond to the gospel?

4. How do we know that the kingdom was established on the day of Pentecost?

5. Who adds people to the church and why is this significant?

4/14/21

6

THE DAY OF JUDGMENT

> *"Therefore having overlooked the times of ignorance, God is now declaring to men that all people everywhere should repent, because He has fixed a day in which He will judge the world in righteousness through a Man whom He has appointed, having furnished proof to all men by raising Him from the dead"* (Acts 17:30-31).

In this sixth lesson, we will be discussing the *day of judgment*. Like the second lesson, this may seem like a bit of a jump to go all the way from the day of Pentecost to here. However, we are not skipping so much as we are going to be summarizing the time between these two days.

The Background

The gospel would go to all the world – Before His ascension, Jesus commissioned His apostles: *"Go into all the world and preach the gospel to all creation"* (Mark 16:15). As we noticed in the previous lesson, the message of the gospel began to be preached on the day of Pentecost to the Jews. However, it would eventually go to the rest of the world as well. Jesus told the apostles that they would be His *"witnesses both in Jerusalem, and in all Judea and Samaria, and even to the remotest part of the earth"* (Acts 1:8).

The saving message of the gospel was first preached to the Gentiles when Peter went to the household of Cornelius. When the apostle arrived, he said, *"I most certainly understand now that God is not one to show partiality, but in every nation the man who fears Him and does what is right is welcome to Him"* (Acts 10:34-35). As he explained what happened to the brethren in Jerusalem, they rightly concluded that *"God has granted to the Gentiles also the repentance that leads to life"* (Acts 11:18).

Approximately thirty years after the church was established in Jerusalem, Paul was able to affirm that the gospel had been *"proclaimed in all creation under heaven"* (Colossians 1:23). This did not mean that every individual heard the gospel; instead, it meant that the message of the gospel was available to everyone.

When Paul spoke to the philosophers that were gathered on Mars Hill in Athens, he said, *"Therefore having overlooked the times of ignorance, God is now declaring to men that all people everywhere should repent"* (Acts 17:30). This is still true today. God is still *"declaring...that all people everywhere should repent"* and is calling us to do so through the gospel.

A certain amount of time would pass – Paul explained that God *"has fixed a day in which He will judge the world in righteousness"* (Acts 17:31). However, even though this day has been *"fixed,"* it has not been revealed when that day will be.

Jesus said, *"But of that day and hour no one knows, not even the angels of heaven, nor the Son, but the Father alone"* (Matthew 24:36).

When Peter wrote about this day, he did not say when it would occur; but he did reveal something about it: *"Know this first of all, that in the last days mockers will come with their mocking, following after their own lusts, and saying, 'Where is the promise of His coming? For ever since the fathers fell asleep, all continues just as it was from the beginning of creation"* (2 Peter 3:3-4). In other words, there would be enough time that would pass to cause some to doubt the promise that the day of the Lord would come.

Life will be going on normally – Again, Peter explained that some would be saying, *"All continues just as it was from the beginning of creation"* (2 Peter 3:4). Of course, these *"mockers"* (2 Peter 3:3) would forget about the destruction of the world in the flood (2 Peter 3:5-6). However, aside from events like this, they were right. Even now, everything does continue as it has because this is how God designed the world to operate (cf. Genesis 8:22). As Paul explained to the residents of Lystra, God's ongoing providence serves as a *"witness"* for Him (Acts 14:17).

Though many want to look for signs that indicate the final day of judgment is approaching, there will be no signs that point to the arrival of this event. Notice what Jesus said about this day:

> *"But of that day and hour no one knows, not even the angels of heaven, nor the Son, but the Father alone. For the coming of the Son of Man will be*

> *just like the days of Noah. For as in those days before the flood they were eating and drinking, marrying and giving in marriage, until the day that Noah entered the ark, and they did not understand until the flood came and took them all away; so will the coming of the Son of Man be"* (Matthew 24:36-39).

The only "signs" that would signal the day of the Lord approaching would be the "signs" that existed during the days of Noah – the righteous making preparations and preaching being done to warn of God's judgment (cf. Hebrews 11:7; 2 Peter 2:5). Peter wrote, *"But the day of the Lord will come like a thief, in which the heavens will pass away with a roar and the elements will be destroyed with intense heat, and the earth and its works will be burned up"* (2 Peter 3:10).

Jesus used this same imagery when He discussed this day: *"Therefore be on the alert, for you do not know which day your Lord is coming. But be sure of this, that if the head of the house had known at what time of the night the thief was coming, he would have been on the alert and would not have allowed his house to be broken into. For this reason you also must be ready; for the Son of Man is coming at an hour when you do not think He will"* (Matthew 24:42-44). Since we do not know when this day will be, we must be prepared for it at all times.

The Events on That Day

The Lord will return from heaven – As we noticed, this day is when *"the Son of Man is coming"* (Matthew 24:44). Jesus is going to return *"in just the same way as* [His apostles] *watched Him go into heaven"* (Acts 1:11). However, the reaction to His return will not be the same for everyone. Notice the following passages:

> *"For the Lord Himself will descend from heaven with a shout, with the voice of the archangel and with the trumpet of God, and the dead in Christ will rise first. Then we who are alive and remain will be caught up together with them in the clouds to meet the Lord in the air, and so we shall always be with the Lord. Therefore comfort one another with these words"* (1 Thessalonians 4:16-18).

> *"The Lord Jesus will be revealed from heaven with His mighty angels in flaming fire, dealing out retribution to those who do not know God and to those who do not obey the gospel of our Lord Jesus. These will pay the penalty of eternal destruction, away from the presence of the Lord and from the glory or His power"* (2 Thessalonians 1:7-9).

> *"It is a terrifying thing to fall into the hands of the living God"* (Hebrews 10:31).

For some, the expectation of Jesus' coming is a source of *comfort*. For others, the prospect of Christ returning in judgment is *terrifying*. The Lord's return will either be a cause of joy or fear, depending on how one has conducted himself in this life.

Everyone will stand before Christ in judgment – Paul explained this in his letter to Corinth: *"For we must all appear before the judgment seat of Christ, so that each one may be recompensed for his deeds in the body, according to what he has done,* *whether good or bad"* (2 Corinthians 5:10). As he explained, we will be judged according to our deeds. This is why God is *"declaring...that all people everywhere should repent"* (Acts 17:30). To prepare for our appointment before the judgment seat of Christ, we must change our lives to make sure our actions are pleasing to Him.

As we understand the reality of the judgment, it is essential that we know what the standard of judgment will be. Jesus said, *"He who rejects Me and does not receive My sayings, has one who judges him; the word I spoke is what will judge him at the last day"* (John 12:48). The word of God that has been revealed to us is the standard by which we will be judged. Therefore, we need to make sure that our deeds are in line with His word.

The righteous and wicked will be separated – Jesus described this when He spoke of the judgment on the final day: *"But when the Son of Man comes in His glory, and all the angels with Him, then He will sit on His glorious throne. All the nations will be gathered before Him; and He will separate them from one another, as the shepherd separates the sheep from the goats; and He will put the sheep on His right, and the goats on the left"* (Matthew 25:31-33).

Sadly, many on the *"left"* will be surprised to be there (cf. Matthew 25:44). In the Sermon on the Mount, after explaining that only those who do the will of the Father will enter heaven (Matthew 7:21), Jesus described the shock that many would have and the plea they would make that there had been some mistake in the Lord's decision: *"Many will say to Me on that day, 'Lord, Lord, did we not prophesy in Your name, and in Your name cast out demons, and in Your name perform many miracles?' And then I will declare to them, 'I never knew you; depart from Me, you who practice lawlessness'"* (Matthew 7:22-23). These individuals were ones who believed in God and attempted to serve Him, yet they would be told to *"depart"* because they were guilty of practicing *"lawlessness."* In other words, they were engaged in practices which had not been commanded or authorized in God's word. The Lord is not going to judge us merely by our intentions but by our actions.

Those who are judged will go either to *"eternal punishment"* or *"eternal life"* (Matthew 25:46), depending on how the Lord judges them to have lived up to His standard.

Key Lessons

Judgment is certain for all men – As we already noticed, Paul wrote, *"For we must all appear before the judgment seat of Christ, so that each one may be recompensed for his deeds in the body, according to what he has done, whether good or bad"* (2 Corinthians 5:10). This judgment is for everyone.

This means that we will not escape from this. Therefore, we must be faithful to the Lord. The Hebrew writer explained the importance of this: *"For if we go on sinning willfully after receiving the knowledge of the truth, there no longer remains a sacrifice for sins, but a terrifying expectation of judgment and the fury of a fire which will consume the adversaries. Anyone who has set aside the Law of Moses dies without mercy on the testimony of two or three witnesses. How much severer punishment do you think he will deserve who has trampled under foot the Son of God, and has regarded as unclean the blood of the covenant by which he was sanctified, and has insulted the Spirit of grace?"* (Hebrews 10:26-29). We often think of the Law of Moses being severe in its punishments. Yet this passage shows us that a *"severer punishment"* than those under the old law is deserved by those who sin against God. The prospect of receiving the full wrath of God ought to be *"a terrifying thing"* to us (Hebrews 10:31). This mental image is not necessarily meant to "scare" us into obedience but to get us realize the great importance of faithfully serving the Lord.

This means that those around us will not escape from this either. Therefore, we must try to reach them with the gospel. In fact, immediately after explaining the certainly of judgment, Paul wrote, *"Therefore, knowing the fear of the Lord, we persuade men"* (2 Corinthians 5:11). Just as we must prepare ourselves for this day, we need to help others see the need to be prepared for themselves.

Judgment will be according to the Lord's standard – Jesus is the one Judge (James 4:12); and His word is the standard (John 12:48). Therefore, it is His word that must be taught. This is why He commissioned His apostles to *"preach the gospel to all creation"* (Mark 16:15). Similarly, we must *"speak as the oracles of God"* (1 Peter 4:11, KJV).

This is also why we are not to judge over matters of opinion or human commandment. Paul told the saints in Rome, *"Now accept the one who is weak in faith, but not for the purpose of passing judgment on his opinions"* (Romans 14:1). Jesus condemned the Pharisees because they were "teaching as doctrines the precepts of men" (Matthew 15:9). What if our opinions seem harmless to us? What if our traditions seem perfectly reasonable? Why could we not preach them anyway? One of the reasons why we must keep from teaching personal opinion or man-made commandments – no matter how "harmless" or "reasonable" they seem to us – is because these do not help anyone prepare for the final judgment since these are not the standard (John 12:48). In fact, teaching those things that are beyond the Scriptures could actually hinder others and put a stumbling block before them. Paul explained, *"Therefore let us not judge one another anymore, but rather determine this—not to put an obstacle or a stumbling block in a brother's way"* (Romans 14:13). We must be content to remain within the bounds of Scripture to prepare ourselves and others for the Lord's judgment.

In looking forward to the day of judgment, John provided some encouragement to those who were following the Lord: *"Now, little children, abide in Him, so that when He appears, we may have confidence and not shrink away from Him in shame at His coming. If you know that He is righteous, you know that everyone also who practices righteousness is born of Him"* (1 John 2:28-29). *"By this, love is perfected with us, so that we may have confidence in the day of judgment; because as He is, so also are we in the world. There is no fear in love; but perfect love casts out fear, because fear involves punishment, and the one who fears is not perfected in love"* (1 John 4:17-18). If we are following the Lord – practicing righteousness and walking in love – we can look forward to His return with confidence, rather than with fear.

Judgment will be final – When we are judged, we will either go to *"eternal punishment"* or *"eternal life"* (Matthew 25:46). These are the only two options. Jesus said, *"Do not marvel at this; for an hour is coming, in which all who are in the tombs will hear His voice, and will come forth; those who did the good deeds to a resurrection of life, those who committed evil deeds to a resurrection of judgment"* (John 5:28-29).

Those who are lost have *"no hope"* (1 Thessalonians 4:13). Instead, what they have to look forward to is worse than anything they could experience in this life. John described this scene: *"And the smoke of their torment goes up forever and ever; they have no rest day and night"* (Revelation 14:11). Everyone should want to do whatever is necessary to avoid this fate.

Those who are saved will "always be with the Lord" (1 Thessalonians 4:17). This means that we, like Paul, should be willing to *"count all things to be loss in view of the surpassing value of knowing Christ Jesus...in order that* [we] *might attain to the resurrection from the dead"* (Philippians 3:8-11).

Conclusion

We do not know when it will be, but we do know that the Lord will return one day to judge the world. He has given us His word (the standard) and the time necessary to prepare. We must use the time we have now to prepare for our appointment before His judgment seat.

Questions for Discussion and Reflection

1. How far would the gospel spread before the day of judgment?

2. What "signs" will indicate that the day of the Lord is approaching?

3. Why will many be surprised to learn their fate?

4. Who will be judged by the Lord in the last day?

5. What is the standard by which we will be judged?

GREAT DAYS IN HISTORY

7

THE DAY OF ETERNITY

"But grow in the grace and knowledge of our Lord and Savior Jesus Christ. To Him be the glory, both now and to the day of eternity. Amen" (2 Peter 3:18).

In the previous lesson we discussed the final day when the Lord will return in judgment. But what happens after life on earth is over? Let us consider what the Bible teaches about the *day of eternity*.

The Background

This world will be destroyed – As we noticed in the previous lesson, the Lord is returning for a final day of judgment in order to judge the world. Regarding this day, Jesus said, *"All the nations will be gathered before Him; and He will separate them from one another"* (Matthew 25:32). After the judgment, the wicked will *"go away into eternal punishment"* and the righteous will go *"into eternal life"* (Matthew 25:46). The wicked will be *"thrown into the lake of fire"* (Revelation

20:15) and *"God will bring with Him those who have fallen asleep in Jesus"* where we will *"always be with the Lord"* (1 Thessalonians 4:14, 17).

We can see from the passages above that the eternal destination for both the righteous and the wicked will be somewhere other than this world. The reason for this is because this world will no longer be here. Notice what Peter wrote:

> *"But the day of the Lord will come like a thief, in which the heavens will pass away with a roar and the elements will be destroyed with intense heat, and the earth and its works will be burned up"* (2 Peter 3:10).

This world is not changing when the Lord returns; it will cease to exist. With this, time will also cease. Time began on the day of Creation (Genesis 1:1-5). However, God – the Creator – is eternal: *"Before the mountains were born or You gave birth to the earth and the world, even from everlasting to everlasting, You are God"* (Psalm 90:2). Before the first day, He had already existed without beginning from eternity. When this world is destroyed, all will return to this existence beyond the bounds of time.

Our bodies will be changed – When Paul wrote to the saints in Corinth about the resurrection, he explained, *"Flesh and blood cannot inherit the kingdom of God"* (1 Corinthians 15:50). Since life after the judgment will last for eternity and our bodies – in their present state – are not designed to last that long, they will have to be changed. Paul continued:

> *"Behold, I tell you a mystery; we will not all sleep, but we will all be changed, in a moment, in the twinkling of an eye, at the last trumpet; for the trumpet will sound, and the dead will be raised imperishable, and we will be changed. For this perishable must put on the imperishable, and this mortal must put on immortality. But when this perishable will have put on the imperishable, and this mortal will have put on immortality, then will come about the saying that is written, 'Death is swallowed up in victory'"* (1 Corinthians 15:51-54).

While John acknowledged that *"it has not appeared as yet what we will be,"* he assured us that when the Lord returns *"we will be like Him, because we will see Him just as He is"* (1 John 3:2). Even the wicked will have bodies that have been changed since *"their torment"* will last *"forever and ever"* (Revelation 14:11) in the place where the *"worm does not die, and the fire is not quenched"* (Mark 9:48). Once we reach the *day of eternity*, our bodies will have been changed into a state which will be suited for those surroundings.

Where we spend eternity will depend upon how we have lived our lives – We discussed this in more detail in the previous lesson. Jesus said, *"Do not marvel at this; for an hour is coming, in which all who are in the tombs will hear His voice, and will come forth; those who did the good deeds to a resurrection of life, those who committed the evil deeds to a resurrection of judgment"* (John 5:28-29). Will we do *"good deeds"* or *"evil deeds"* while here on the earth?

The Events on That Day

The wicked will face eternal torment – In describing the fate of those who would be punished by the Lord when He returns, Paul wrote, *"These will pay the penalty of eternal destruction, away from the presence of the Lord and from the glory of His power"* (2 Thessalonians 1:9). Jude explained that the destruction of Sodom and Gomorrah served as *"an example in undergoing the punishment of eternal fire"* (Jude 7).

Some have the misguided notion that hell can be enjoyed. They think of it as the domain of Satan; therefore, since the devil tempts us with things we might enjoy in this life, they believe we will find enjoyment there. However, hell is not the domain of Satan. Paul described the devil as *"the god of this world"* (2 Corinthians 4:4). His domain is here, not in hell. Hell has been prepared not as a place for Satan to rule but for him to be punished. Jesus explained that this place of *"eternal fire"* had been *"prepared for the devil and his angels"* (Matthew 25:41).

There is no reason for us to want to go to this place of punishment – not even for the company. Many rationalize that they should prefer to go to hell because their friends and family will be there. However, Jesus told of a rich man who found himself in a place of torment after death, and he wanted to send a message to his brothers to warn them not to come to the same place (Luke 16:27-28). The prospect of being in that place with his loved ones was no comfort to him.

The righteous will be in the presence of God – After *"the dead in Christ...rise,"* Paul said that those *"who are alive and remain will be caught up together with them in the clouds to meet the Lord in the air, and so we shall always be with the Lord"* (1

Thessalonians 4:16-17). The promise of being with God for eternity was something that would provide *"comfort"* for the brethren in Thessalonica and for us today. John described the scene in heaven as a place of paradise in the presence of God:

> *"There will no longer be any curse; and the throne of God and of the Lamb will be in it, and His bond-servants will serve Him; they will see His face, and His name will be on their foreheads. And there will no longer be any night; and they will not have need of the light of a lamp nor the light of the sun, because the Lord God will illumine them; and they will reign forever and ever"* (Revelation 22:3-5).

When the righteous reach this home with the Lord, they will be comforted after enduring all of the hardships of this life: *"And He will wipe away every tear from their eyes; and there will no longer be any death; there will no longer be any mourning, or crying, or pain; the first things have passed away"* (Revelation 21:4).

The righteous will enjoy rest – John wrote, *"And I heard a voice from heaven, saying, 'Write, "Blessed are the dead who die in the Lord from now on!"' 'Yes,' says the Spirit, 'so that they may rest from their labors, for their deeds follow with them'"* (Revelation 14:13). However, the fact that those who *"die in the Lord"* will enjoy *"rest"* implies that we are to be working for the Lord now. Those who belong to the Lord are to be *"zealous for good deeds"* (Titus 2:14).

Key Lessons

God will reward those who follow Him – As we have

already seen, those who *"die in the Lord"* are blessed because *"their deeds follow with them"* (Revelation 14:13). These are the ones who have practiced *"good deeds"* leading to *"a resurrection of life"* (John 5:29). Those who follow the Lord will be rewarded by Him.

> *"He who loves his life loses it, and he who hates his life in this world will keep it to life eternal. If anyone serves Me, he must follow Me; and where I am, there My servant will be also; if anyone serves Me, the Father will honor him"* (John 12:25-26).

Jesus told His disciples, *"Do not let your heart be troubled; believe in God, believe also in Me. In My Father's house are many dwelling places; if it were not so, I would have told you; for I go to prepare a place for you. If I go and prepare a place for you, I will come again and receive you to Myself, that where I am, there you may be also"* (John 14:1-3). This promise was not just to the ones who would be commissioned as His apostles. Rather, this promise is for all of us. Jesus is *"to all those who obey Him the source of eternal salvation"* (Hebrews 5:9). The Hebrew writer also said, *"And without faith it is impossible to please Him, for he who comes to God must believe that He is and that He is a rewarder of those who seek Him"* (Hebrews 11:6). We must have faith that the Lord will reward us with an eternal home in heaven with Him.

God will punish those who refuse to follow Him – In describing the final judgment against the wicked, Paul explained that Jesus will return *"dealing out retribution to those who do not know God and to those who do not obey the gospel of our Lord Jesus. These will pay the penalty of eternal destruction, away from the presence of the Lord and from the glory of His power"* (2

Thessalonians 1:8-9).

Throughout the Old Testament, God has shown His willingness and ability to punish those who were disobedient. Paul highlighted several examples of this with God's own people when he wrote to the church in Corinth:

> *"Nevertheless, with most of them God was not well-pleased; for they were laid low in the wilderness. Now these things happened as examples for us, so that we would not crave evil things as they also craved. Do not be idolaters, as some of them were; as it is written, 'The people sat down to eat and drink, and stood up to play.' Nor let us act immorally, as some of them did, and twenty-three thousand fell in one day. Nor let us try the Lord, as some of them did, and were destroyed by the serpents. Nor grumble, as some of them did, and were destroyed by the destroyer. Now these things happened to them as an example, and they were written for our instruction, upon whom the ends of the ages have come"* (1 Corinthians 10:5-11).

Since God is willing and able to punish those who do not submit to His will, we must fear Him. Jesus said, *"Do not fear those who kill the body but are unable to kill the soul; but rather fear Him who is able to destroy both soul and body in hell"* (Matthew 10:28). Right now, God is being patient with us, giving us time to make our lives right with Him. He is *"not wishing for any to perish but for all to come to repentance"* (2 Peter 3:9).

However, we need to be sure we are taking advantage of His patience. There is a temptation to respond to God's longsuffering with a casual attitude toward sin, concluding that we will always have time later to make corrections. Yet Paul warned, *"Or do you think lightly of the riches of His kindness and tolerance and patience, not knowing that the kindness of God leads you to repentance?"* (Romans 2:4). We are not to *"continue in sin so that grace may increase,"* but instead we must *"consider* [ourselves] *to be dead to sin, but alive to God in Christ Jesus"* (Romans 6:1, 11).

This is for eternity – As we discussed in the previous lesson, judgment is *final* (Matthew 25:46). Whatever hardships we face in this life are short by comparison. Paul wrote, *"For momentary, light affliction is producing for us an eternal weight of glory far beyond all comparison"* (2 Corinthians 4:17). Despite the severe hardships Paul faced in this life (2 Corinthians 11:23-29), he was able to refer to all of these things as *"light affliction"* in view of eternity.

Whatever pleasure we experience from sin is fleeting. Moses recognized this and, therefore, was willing to *"endure ill-treatment with the people of God* [rather] *than to enjoy the passing pleasures of sin"* (Hebrews 11:25). Because everything in this life is temporary, we must not allow *anything* in this life (good or bad) to hinder us from serving the Lord.

This has always been God's plan – God chose to redeem a people for Himself *"before the foundation of the world"* (Ephesians 1:4). The sacrifice of Christ on the cross, which was necessary in order to redeem us from sin, was likewise known beforehand. John referred to Jesus as *"the Lamb slain from the foundation of the world"* (Revelation 13:8, KJV). Before time began, God's intention was to have a people with Him for eternity.

We usually think of this world's history as being so long and vast, yet it is just a blip in God's eternal purpose. As Paul wrote to the church in Ephesus about *"the mystery"* that was given to him *"by revelation,"* (Ephesians 3:3), he explained that God's *"eternal purpose* [was] *carried out in Christ Jesus our Lord"* (Ephesians 3:11). Many people think of God's purpose being to bless them in this life. While He certainly does bless us here (cf. Acts 14:16-17; James 1:17), the Scriptures teach that His plan since the beginning has been to deliver us through this life on earth into eternal life in heaven.

Conclusion

We think of everything in this life in terms of *time* (when, how long, until, etc.). Yet time is temporary. There is a *day of eternity* that awaits us. No matter what happens in our time on earth, we need to make sure we are preparing for what is coming next.

Questions for Discussion and Reflection

1. What will happen to this world when the Lord returns?

2. Why must our bodies be changed?

3. Describe the eternal fate of the wicked.

4. Describe the eternal fate of the righteous.

5. Knowing that our fate after the judgment is eternal, how should be view our lives here?

8

TODAY

> *"For we have become partakers of Christ, if we hold fast the beginning of our assurance firm until the end, while it is said, 'Today if you hear His voice, do not harden your hearts, as when they provoked Me'"* (Hebrews 3:14-15).

In this final lesson, we are not going to keep moving further down a timeline. There is nothing past the *day of eternity*. Instead, we are going to talk about *today* to see what we need to do with what we have learned in this series.

The Background

We have experienced God's blessings in this life – James wrote, *"Every good thing given and every perfect gift is from above, coming down from the Father of lights, with whom there is no variation or shifting shadow"* (James 1:17). Though the context was specifically addressing the fact that God will not lead us to sin (James 1:13-16), the principle applies broadly. Everything good that is available to us has been made possible by God.

However, experiencing God's blessings in this life is not a perk exclusively for Christians. Jesus explained that both the righteous and the wicked receive God's blessings: *"He causes His sun to rise on the evil and the good, and sends rain on the righteous and the unrighteous"* (Matthew 5:45). The blessings that we receive from God and the goodness we experience in this life should lead us to put our trust in Him. Paul told Timothy, *"Instruct those who are rich in this present world not to be conceited or to fix their hope on the uncertainty of riches, but on God, who richly supplies us with all things to enjoy"* (1 Timothy 6:17). Since God has richly blessed us, we should respond by doing *"good"* and being *"rich in good works"* (1 Timothy 6:18).

We have also experienced hardships in this life – Even though God richly blesses us in this life, not everything that we experience is good or pleasant. Job said, *"Man, who is born of woman, is short-lived and full of turmoil"* (Job 14:1).

Just as God's blessings are given to both Christians and non-Christians, both the righteous and the wicked will also experience hardships in this life. On one hand, the wicked will often suffer as a result of their sin. The wise man noted this: *"Good understanding produces favor, but the way of the treacherous is hard"* (Proverbs 13:15). However, there are also times in which the righteous suffer in the same way that the wicked suffer even though they do not commit the same sins. *"There is futility which is done on the earth, that is, there are righteous men to whom it happens according to the deeds of the wicked"* (Ecclesiastes 8:14). Yet regardless of who faces these trials, the suffering should cause us to turn to God. The Lord said, *"Call upon Me in the day of trouble; I shall rescue you, and you will honor Me"* (Psalm 50:15). Both experience and divinely-inspired Scripture show us that *all people* will suffer hardships and trials

in this life.

God did everything necessary to make salvation possible – Paul told Titus that God made salvation available to everyone: *"For the grace of God has appeared, bringing salvation to all men"* (Titus 2:11). Jesus used a parable to indicate that preparations have been made to bring about this salvation:

> *"The kingdom of heaven may be compared to a king who gave a wedding feast for his son. And he sent out his slaves to call those who had been invited to the wedding feast, and they were unwilling to come. Again he sent out other slaves saying, 'Tell those who have been invited, "Behold, I have prepared my dinner; my oxen and my fattened livestock are all butchered and everything is ready; come to the wedding feast"'"* (Matthew 22:2-4).

This series has been about the plan that God carried out to bring salvation to men:

1. He created a perfect world and then, after the world was marred by sin, delivered a prophecy that promised the coming of Christ to defeat sin and the devil.
2. He made a promise to Abraham that through his seed the world would be blessed, then preserved that seed in the nation of Israel through generations.
3. He sent His Son – Jesus Christ – to earth in order to suffer and die on the cross for our sins.
4. He raised Jesus from the dead, proving Him

to be the Son of God and giving hope for those who would faithfully serve Him.

5. He established the church and a plan whereby the saving message of the gospel could be spread.

God did everything that was required to make salvation available for us. Nothing was left undone that needed to be carried out.

The Events on That Day

Life goes on as it always does – Today, just as it was in the day which Peter wrote, everything *"continues just as it was from the beginning of creation"* (2 Peter 3:4). Though *"mockers"* will use this fact to ridicule the idea of the Lord returning (2 Peter 3:3), we understand this to be a proof of God's providence as it represents the continued fulfillment of the promise to Noah: *"While the earth remains, seedtime and harvest, and cold and heat, and summer and winter, and day and night shall not cease"* (Genesis 8:22). However, everything continuing in this way is not just until the end draws near; it will continue up until the moment the Lord returns. Notice what Jesus said:

> *"But of that day and hour no one knows, not even the angels of heaven, nor the Son, but the Father alone. For the coming of the Son of Man will be just like the days of Noah. For as in those days before the flood they were eating and drinking, marrying and giving in marriage, until the day that Noah entered the ark, and they did not understand until the flood came and took them all away; so will the coming of the Son of Man be. [...] Therefore be on the alert, for*

> *you do not know which day your Lord is coming*" (Matthew 24:36-42).

While there were warning signs that signaled the coming destruction of Jerusalem (Matthew 24:4-35), Jesus explained that there would be no such signs at the end of the world. Life would go on as normal, just like it had in the days of Noah before the flood. The only "signs" that warned of the end were Noah's preaching (2 Peter 2:5) and preparations being made by God's people (Hebrews 11:7). The same is true today. Though people may look for various signs that indicate the end is close, the only "signs" are the gospel being preached and Christians preparing for the Lord's return.

Part of the fact that life will go on as normal means that we will continue to face hardships in this life. As we already noticed, Job articulated the reality that all of us experience: "*Man, who is born of woman, is short-lived and full of turmoil*" (Job 14:1). Yet these trials should only make us long for our reward in heaven. Paul wrote, "*For I consider the sufferings of this present time are not worthy to be compared with the glory that is to be revealed to us*" (Romans 8:18). Despite the fact that he faced intense hardships, the apostle was able to describe his sufferings as "*momentary, light affliction*" when he compared it with the "*eternal weight of glory*" which will be experienced after this life (2 Corinthians 4:17-18).

God continues to be patient – This patience is not to be interpreted as God condoning sin, but it is to give us time to repent. Paul explained this when he wrote to the saints in Rome: "*Or do you think lightly of the riches of His kindness and tolerance and patience, not knowing that the kindness of God leads you to repentance?*" (Romans 2:4). We should not remain in sin because God is patient; instead, we should repent of sin in the time we have been afforded by His patience.

We should remember what the Bible says about sin: *"For the wages of sin is death, but the free gift of God is eternal life in Christ Jesus our Lord"* (Romans 6:23). This *"death"* is not physical death but is eternal separation from God. Not only must we understand the "wages of sin," we also need to realize the universal problem of sin: *"For all have sinned and fall short of the glory of God"* (Romans 3:23). Every one of us has sinned and, therefore, deserves the punishment that comes as a result.

If we have all sinned and eternal destruction is the punishment, why has this not happened yet? It is because God wants us to repent: *"The Lord is not slow about His promise, as some count slowness, but is patient toward you, not wishing for any to perish but for all to come to repentance"* (2 Peter 3:9). As the Lord said through the prophet, *"For I have no pleasure in the death of anyone who dies... Therefore, repent and live"* (Ezekiel 18:32). God wants us to be saved and avoid the punishment that comes with sin. Therefore, He continues to be patient to give us time to repent.

We will make choices regarding our conduct and manner of life – Joshua told the Israelites, *"Choose for yourselves today whom you will serve...but as for me and my house, we will serve the Lord"* (Joshua 24:15). In the same way, we must choose what we will do in this life. We have many different options as to how we will live our lives. The wise man said, *"Many plans are in a man's heart, but the counsel of the Lord will stand"* (Proverbs 19:21). Our plans are many, but they do not change God's word. This is why *persuasion* is used to lead us to obey the

Lord (2 Corinthians 5:11). We must make the choice for ourselves – based upon the incentives that God has revealed to us in His word – to repent of our sins and serve Him so that we can reach the reward of heaven.

Key Lessons

Now is the time to prepare – Paul told the brethren in Corinth, *"For He says, 'At the acceptable time I listened to you, and on the day of salvation I helped you.' Behold, now is 'the acceptable time,' behold, now is 'the day of salvation'"* (2 Corinthians 6:2). While God continues to be patient in order to give us time to repent (Romans 2:4), one day His patience will no longer be extended. The reality is that we have no promise of tomorrow. Consider what James wrote on this:

> *"Come now, you who say, 'Today or tomorrow we will go to such and such a city, and spend a year there and engage in business and make a profit.' Yet you do not know what your life will be like tomorrow. You are just a vapor that appears for a little while and then vanishes away"* (James 4:13-14).

In the parable of a rich land owner, Jesus described one who believed he had plenty of time to take care of his soul later: *"'And I will say to my soul, "Soul, you have many goods laid up for many years to come; take your ease, eat, drink, and be merry."' But God said to him, 'You fool! This very night your soul is required of you; and now who will own what you have prepared?'"* (Luke 12:19-20). Jesus made it clear that it is *foolish* to put off preparing our souls for eternity. The time to prepare is *today*.

Therefore, we cannot allow tomorrow to distract us from where our focus needs to be. Jesus said, *"But seek first His kingdom and His righteousness, and all these things will be added to you. So do not worry about tomorrow; for tomorrow will care for itself. Each day has enough trouble of its own"* (Matthew 6:33-34). Our priority for each day must be doing what is necessary to be pleasing to the Lord and serving Him faithfully in His kingdom.

Our past does not have to hinder us – As Paul looked forward with anticipation to the hope of the resurrection, he wrote, *"Brethren, I do not regard myself as having laid hold of it yet; but one thing I do: forgetting what lies behind and reaching forward to what lies ahead, I press on toward the goal for the prize of the upward call of God in Christ Jesus"* (Philippians 3:13-14). Because the reward was in the future, he was determined to not let anything hinder him from reaching it – including his past. In the same way, we must not allow our past to hinder our pursuit of the goal of heaven.

- No matter what sins we have committed in the past, we can start living righteously *today* – Paul was *"formerly a blasphemer and a persecutor and a violent aggressor"* and was the *"foremost of all"* sinners, yet he was *"shown mercy"* and was able to be saved and serve the Lord (1 Timothy 1:12-15). This was *"an example"* to show that anyone can be saved, regardless of his past, if he will serve the Lord as Paul did.
- No matter how much time we have wasted in the past, we can begin serving God *today* – In the parable of the laborers in the vineyard,

Jesus explained that those who were hired at *"the eleventh hour"* received the same reward as those who worked from the start of the day (Matthew 20:1-16). His point was that it is never too late for one to start serving the Lord.

- No matter what good we have done in the past, we must continue serving the Lord *today* – This is also important for us to remember. Paul recognized that though he was faithfully serving the Lord, even he as an apostle could *"be disqualified"* if he did not continue run the race before him (1 Corinthians 9:24-27). The same is true for us. We must remain faithful throughout our lives (Revelation 2:10).

We cannot afford to let anything from our past keep us from the future happiness and security in heaven.

We must decide what we will do – We already noticed the challenge issued by Joshua: *"Choose for yourselves today whom you will serve"* (Joshua 24:15). No one can make the choice for us. Each one of us will make our own decision. We need to realize that not making a commitment to serve the Lord is a decision in itself. Making a decision is not just something that we ought to do but is something that we most certainly will do. Therefore, we need to be sure we make the right decision.

Conclusion

God's eternal purpose has been to save a people for Himself. As we have studied in this series of lessons, He has done everything necessary to make that salvation possible.

Now it is up to us to take advantage of the salvation that He offers.

> *"Behold, now is 'the acceptable time,' behold, now is 'the day of salvation'"* (2 Corinthians 6:2).

Today is the day be right with the Lord.

Questions for Discussion and Reflection

1. What have all people experienced in life?

2. Why has God allowed the earth to remain as long as it has?

3. Why is "today" the right time to prepare for eternity?

4. What are some ways that we could let our past hinder us and why should we not allow this to happen?

5. Who is responsible for us making the decision to serve the Lord?

69503472R00059

Made in the USA
Columbia, SC
15 August 2019